Baltimore and the Nineteenth of April, 1861

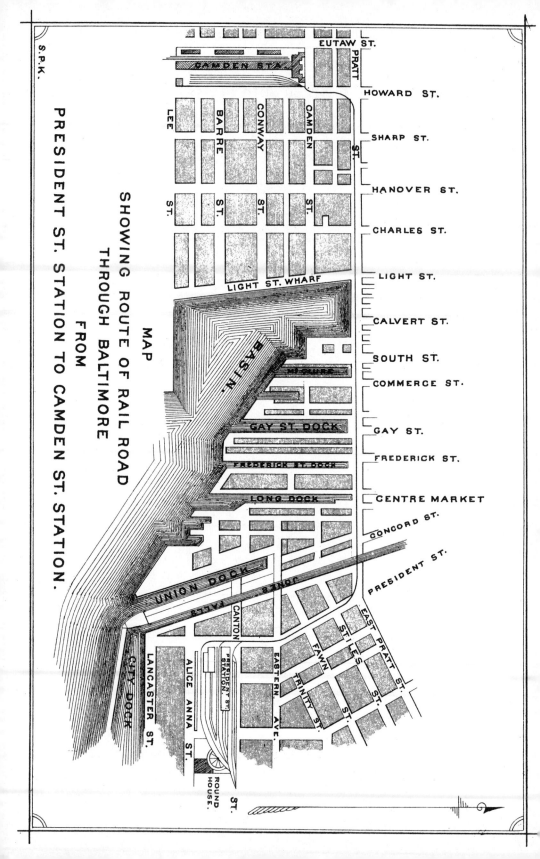

MAP

SHOWING ROUTE OF RAIL ROAD

THROUGH BALTIMORE

FROM

PRESIDENT ST. STATION TO CAMDEN ST. STATION.

S.P.K.

EUTAW ST.

PRATT ST.

CAMDEN STA.

HOWARD ST.

SHARP ST.

HANOVER ST.

CHARLES ST.

LIGHT ST.

CALVERT ST.

SOUTH ST.

COMMERCE ST.

GAY ST.

FREDERICK ST.

CENTRE MARKET

CONCORD ST.

PRESIDENT ST.

EAST PRATT ST.

LEE ST.

BARRE ST.

CONWAY ST.

CAMDEN ST.

LIGHT ST. WHARF

BASIN

M. DOCK

GAY ST. DOCK

FREDERICK ST. DOCK

LONG DOCK

UNION DOCK

FALLS BRANCH

CANTON ST.

PRESIDENT ST. STATION

ALICE ANNA ST.

LANCASTER ST.

CITY DOCK

EASTERN AVE.

FAWN ST.

TRINITY ST.

STILES ST.

ROUND HOUSE.

BALTIMORE

AND

THE NINETEENTH OF APRIL, 1861

A Study of the War

By GEORGE WILLIAM BROWN

Chief Judge of the Supreme Bench of Baltimore, and Mayor of the City in 1861

WITH A NEW INTRODUCTION
BY KEVIN CONLEY RUFFNER

THE JOHNS HOPKINS UNIVERSITY PRESS
BALTIMORE AND LONDON

Originally published by N. Murray, Publication Agent, Johns Hopkins
University, 1887
Johns Hopkins Paperbacks edition, 2001
9 8 7 6 5 4 3 2 1

The Johns Hopkins University Press
2715 North Charles Street
Baltimore, Maryland 21218-4363
www.press.jhu.edu

Library of Congress Cataloging-in-Publication Data

Brown, George William, 1812–1890.
    Baltimore and the nineteenth of April, 1861 : a study of the war / by
George William Brown.
        p.   cm.
    Originally published: Baltimore : N. Murray, 1887, in series:
Johns Hopkins University studies in historical and political science.
Extra volume ; 3.
    Includes bibliographical references and index.
    ISBN 0-8018-6724-X (pbk. : acid-free paper)
    1. Baltimore (Md.)—History—Civil War, 1861–1865. 2. Baltimore
(Md.)—History—Civil War, 1861–1865—Personal narratives. 3. Baltimore
(Md.)—History—Civil War, 1861–1865—Social aspects. 4. Riots—
Maryland—Baltimore—History—19th century. 5. Secession—Maryland.
6. Brown, George William, 1812–1890. 7. Mayors—Maryland—
Baltimore—Biography. 8. United States—History—Civil War, 1861–
1865—Personal narratives. 9. United States—History—Civil War, 1861–
1865—Social aspects. 10. United States—Politics and government—
1861–1865. I. Title: Baltimore and the 19th of April, 1861. II. Title.

F189.B157 B76 2001
975.2'7103—dc21   2001018658

A catalog volume of this book is available from the British Library.

INTRODUCTION TO THE 2001 EDITION.

Few Marylanders better represent the tragedy that befell the state of Maryland in the mid-nineteenth century than George William Brown. As mayor of Baltimore in 1861, Brown was helpless to prevent the breakup of the United States; and he suffered much in the ensuing conflict. His account of those climatic days on the local level is both heartrending and insightful. It serves as a reminder of what can happen when passion overtakes reason and when normal social and political ties are stretched beyond the breaking point.

Not until 1887 did Brown feel that he could record his memories of how the Civil War came to Maryland; and even then he stepped carefully. As he wrote in the first chapter of *Baltimore and the Nineteenth of April, 1861*, "it is not pleasant to disturb the ashes of a great conflagration"; the cold surface concealed "embers still capable of emitting both smoke and heat." Brown took up his pen because he realized that he was among the last living members of his generation who could describe the events that took place in Baltimore. "But more than twenty-five years have passed, and with them have passed away most of the generation then living; as one of the rapidly diminishing survivors, I am admonished by the lengthening shadows that anything I may have to say should be said speedily." Fortunately for those interested in Maryland's history and her role in the Civil War, Brown heeded his own advice; within three years of the book's publication, he was dead.

How did George William Brown arrive upon the stage in 1861 and what role did he play at the outbreak of the Civil War? Born in Baltimore on October 13, 1812, Brown was the

son of George John Brown, a city merchant, and Esther
Allison. His paternal grandfather, Dr. George Brown, was born
in Ireland, studied medicine at the University of Edinburgh,
and settled in Baltimore in 1783. On his mother's side,
Brown's grandfather, Rev. Dr. Patrick Allison, was the first
minister of Baltimore's First Presbyterian Church.[1]

Reflective of his status as a member of Baltimore's gentry,
Brown received a classical secondary education at the Baltimore City College and attended Dartmouth College for his
undergraduate studies. Forced to leave school upon the death
of his father, Brown returned to his studies and graduated
from New Jersey's Rutgers College in 1831 at the head of his
class. That same year, he read law in the offices of Judge
Pruviance and was admitted to the Baltimore Bar shortly
afterwards. In 1839 Brown joined with Frederick W. Brune, a
former classmate and an old friend, to establish a law practice
in Baltimore, a partnership that prospered over the decades to
become Baltimore's oldest firm. Brown married Clara Maria
Brune, the sister of his partner, later that year. The couple
eventually had seven children.

Brown became increasingly active in Baltimore affairs as
Maryland underwent political, social, and economic upheavals
during the first half of the nineteenth century. The impending
expiration of the Second Bank of the United States' charter in
1836 prompted a contentious debate between President Andrew Jackson and Congress. In 1831, Jackson vetoed a bill to
renew the bank's charter and this became a leading issue
during the 1832 presidential campaign. After his reelection,
Jackson wanted to destroy the bank through the withdrawal of

[1] Biographical details about Brown's life are found in a variety of newspaper
clippings located in the Dielman-Hayward File at the Maryland Historical Society, Baltimore, Md. The clippings were drawn from unidentified Baltimore newspapers and other miscellaneous sources.

federal deposits. In a controversial move, Jackson redirected federal deposits from the central bank to some twenty-three state-chartered banks, the so-called "pet banks."

In the meantime, the national bank crisis brought about the collapse of several Maryland banks, including the Bank of Maryland, in 1834. By the following year, many Marylanders faced financial ruin as deposits disappeared with no hope of recovery. On August 6, 1835, a small group of Baltimoreans attacked the residence of Reverdy Johnson, one of the Bank of Maryland's trustees. After a quick appeal from Baltimore Mayor Jesse Hunt, the group dispersed and Mayor Hunt called for a series of public meetings to discuss the bank's problems. For the next several days, the threat of mob action against the Bank of Maryland hung in the air. On August 8, rioting broke out in Baltimore's Monument Square. Unable to attack Johnson's guarded residence, the rioters turned their attention to the house of another bank trustee and ransacked it.[2]

Volunteer citizen guards and police forces opened fire on the rioters, but the violence continued the next evening when Johnson's house and other property were also pillaged. Baltimore appeared on the verge of anarchy with the city's government helpless to protect life and property. Federal forces rushed to the city while General Samuel Smith, a hero of the War of 1812, rallied Baltimoreans to suppress the mob action. Twenty-two-year-old George William Brown answered General Smith's call and served as a volunteer during Baltimore's long, hot summer of 1835.

---

[2] A description of the Bank Riots and the events leading up to the breakdown of law and order in Baltimore can be found in J. Thomas Scharf, *History of Maryland from the Earliest Period to the Present Day* (Baltimore: J. B. Piet, 1879; reprint ed., Hatboro: Tradition Press, 1967), 3:176–82; and David Grimsted, *American Mobbing, 1828–1861: Toward Civil War* (New York: Oxford Univ. Press, 1998).

Seven years later, Brown opposed restrictions on the right of Marylanders to manumit slaves. An Annapolis convention of Maryland slaveowners in January 1842 proposed several measures, including an act requiring all free blacks to leave Maryland. Brown rejected these steps as both unjust and impracticable. Brown, like many Marylanders, recognized the growing role of free black labor in Maryland's economy as slavery slowly diminished in both numbers and importance.

Baltimore's meteoric rise to become the nation's third largest city by 1860 was not without growing pains. Just prior to the outbreak of the Civil War, Baltimore had over 200,000 residents, an enormous jump from the city's population of just 13,000 in 1790. The massive influx of immigrants between 1830 and 1860 fueled a large portion of Baltimore's growth.[3] Of the city's 52,000 immigrants in 1860, most hailed from Ireland and Germany. Baltimore also counted a sizable population of free blacks, some 25,000, and slightly more than 2,000 slaves.

Unique among American antebellum cities, the mixture of white immigrants and free blacks created fierce competition in the marketplace. Coupled with Baltimore's unusual social position, the city also stood out for several other reasons. The state's 1851 constitution altered traditional political align-

---

[3] General references for Maryland's political and social antebellum history include Jean H. Baker, *Ambivalent Americans: The Know-Nothing Party in Maryland* (Baltimore: Johns Hopkins Univ. Press, 1977); and idem., *The Politics of Continuity: Maryland Political Parties from 1858 to 1870* (Baltimore: Johns Hopkins Univ. Press, 1973); Gary Lawson Browne, *Baltimore in the Nation, 1789–1861* (Chapel Hill: Univ. of North Carolina Press, 1980); Robert J. Brugger, *Maryland: A Middle Temperament, 1634–1980* (Baltimore: Johns Hopkins Univ. Press, 1988); William J. Evitts, *A Matter of Allegiances: Maryland from 1850 to 1861* (Baltimore: Johns Hopkins Univ. Press, 1974); and Barbara Jeanne Fields, *Slavery and Freedom on the Middle Ground: Maryland during the Nineteenth Century* (New Haven: Yale Univ. Press, 1985).

ments in Maryland, and, on the national front, the struggle over the Compromise of 1850 gravely injured Maryland's political equilibrium. The subsequent dissolution of the Whig Party in the 1852 national elections left many Marylanders in the lurch. These voters turned to prohibition and nativism as answers to the problems facing their communities. By 1854, the Know-Nothing, or American, Party seized the reins of mayoral power in Baltimore, marking the rise of one of America's most unusual third parties.

By the mid-1850s, Baltimore's seething ethnic cauldron had become incorporated into larger struggles for political dominance. The previously Democratic strongholds of central Maryland and Baltimore had now become bastions for the Know-Nothings, while southern Maryland, long the domain of the Whig Party, had turned Democratic as that party became the defender of the rights of slaveholders. In 1855, the Know-Nothings nearly completed their sweep to power in Maryland by capturing the Baltimore City Council chambers, the legislature in Annapolis, and the majority of Maryland's seats in the U.S. House of Representatives.

To solidify its political base, the Know-Nothings shifted from an anti-immigrant stance to a vague conception of Unionism. In the meantime, the party used the spoils system and the politics of violence to maintain control. Baltimore, whose reputation as a town of roughs long predated the Bank Riots of 1835, experienced high levels of violence throughout the 1850s.[4] The Know-Nothings projected its strong-arm image through volunteer fire companies and gangs, while the Democrats organized political clubs among the various immigrant

---

[4] For example, see Amy Sophia Greenberg, "Mayhem in Mobtown: Firefighting in Antebellum Baltimore," *Maryland Historical Magazine* 90 (Summer 1995): 164–79.

groups. As Jean Baker has noted, "the uses of violence were too rewarding for political leaders, too therapeutic for participants, and too institutionalized for society to stop."[5]

The 1856 presidential elections, the 1857 congressional elections, and the 1858 Baltimore mayoral elections all solidified the Know-Nothing stranglehold in Baltimore and in Maryland at large. Election days were violent affairs as Know-Nothing groups, known by such colorful names as the Blood Tubs, Red Necks, Pioneers, Ashlands, Spartans, Rip Raps, Plug Uglies, Regulators, Black Snakes, Tigers, Eubolts, Gladiators, Ranters, and Little Fellows, took to the streets to enforce Know-Nothing rule. Political violence reigned in a city wracked by day-to-day violence. Police protection in Baltimore was notably weak and ineffective, Election Day or not.

In this troubled atmosphere, George William Brown rose to the forefront among Baltimore's citizens tired of the bloodshed and corruption. In November 1858, Brown joined other notable Baltimoreans to establish the City Reform Association to combat political violence. Although they were defeated in the 1859 elections, the association laid the seed for the Maryland legislature's action the following year. The Democrats, eager to attack the Know-Nothings, used reform as a means to seize control of the General Assembly. The new legislature in early 1860 refused to seat any member of the American Party who obtained his seat through illegal means. The state legislature, in turn, declared the Baltimore city elections in November 1859 to be null and void. Likewise, the House of Delegates adopted the platform of the City Reform Association to strip the Know-Nothings of their power by reorganizing the Baltimore police and improving election procedures and jury selection. As a result, the Know-Nothings

---

[5] Baker, *Ambivalent Americans,* 129–34.

were effectively shut out of power in Maryland at the same time their short-lived party dissolved on the national level.

George William Brown first made his mark as a reformer in March 1853 when he delivered an address to the Maryland Institute. His speech, "Lawlessness, the Evil of the Day," attacked social unrest and party violence. Brown advocated the establishment of professional police and fire departments in Baltimore; the sentencing of juvenile delinquents to the House of Reform as opposed to prison; the end of "straw bail"; and tougher punishments for adult criminals. Brown also advocated stricter rules for the pardoning of criminals. The reforms called for by Brown in 1853 served as the basis for the City Reform Association's platform in 1859.

In August 1860, a committee of citizens nominated George William Brown as its candidate for the office of Baltimore mayor. "A gentleman not only worthy of the fullest confidence in virtue of his irreproachable private character and acknowledged ability," according to one contemporary Maryland historian, "but especially entitled to the respect of his fellow citizens, by his manly stand he took at the municipal elections of 1859. Without partisan motives or objects to induce him to incur unnecessary risks," Brown put "himself in the front ranks of those who endeavored to hold in check the ruffians who surrounded the tenth ward polls. Deeming it incumbent on him to assist in protecting the rights of the humblest and weakest of his fellow citizens, he threw himself into the midst of his assailants, and endured such outrages and insults as few men would have cared to face."[6]

The elections held on October 10, 1860, were described as "quiet as a Sunday," with none of the upheavals of previous years. George William Brown swept into power with over

---

[6] Scharf, *History of Maryland,* 3:283–84.

17,000 votes, while his Know-Nothing opponent, Samuel Hindes, received only 9,000 votes. "Mr. Brown headed a ticket which personified and embodied the enforcement of laws, the safety of society and the divorce of the city government from party politics." In contrast, "those opposed to him and the other reform nominees were classed as the advocates of disorder, of the tainted ballot-box and a perverted and partisan municipality." The 1860 election of George William Brown to mayor of Baltimore marked the beginning of the end of a long streak of political violence, perhaps unique in American political history. "The cause of right triumphed and the final measure of reform which placed the government of Baltimore in hands worthy to administer it was consummated."[7]

George William Brown's term as mayor, however, was soon overshadowed by the Civil War.[8] He soon faced his greatest political and personal challenges over the next two years—a period in which he witnessed the most historic bloodletting on

---

[7] Ibid., 284–85.

[8] For background on the Baltimore riots of April 1861 and various interpretations, see Robert I. Cottom Jr. and Mary Ellen Hayward, *Maryland in the Civil War: A House Divided* (Baltimore: Maryland Historical Society, 1994), 29–32; Harold R. Manakee, *Maryland in the Civil War* (Baltimore: Maryland Historical Society, 1961), 30–38; Matthew Ellenberger, "Whigs in the Streets? Baltimore Republicanism in the Spring of 1861," *Maryland Historical Magazine* 86 (Spring 1991): 39–50; Charles B. Clark, "Baltimore and the Attack on the Sixth Massachusetts Regiment, April 19, 1861," *Maryland Historical Magazine* 56 (March 1961): 39–71; Charles McHenry Howard, "Baltimore and the Crisis of 1861," *Maryland Historical Magazine* 41 (December 1946): 257–81; Frank Towers, ed., "Military Waif: A Sidelight in the Baltimore Riot of 19 April 1861," *Maryland Historical Magazine* 89 (Winter 1994): 427–46; Frank Towers, "'A Vociferous Army of Howling Wolves': Baltimore's Civil War Riot of April 19, 1861," *Maryland Historian* 23 (Fall/Winter 1992): 1–27; and idem., "Maryland's Secessionist Moment: April 1861," (paper presented at the Evergreen House, Baltimore, Md., January 22, 1995).

Baltimore streets. He walked a tight rope between the pressure at home and from officials (including President Abraham Lincoln) in Washington, D.C., to prevent a full-scale uprising.

Brown's *Baltimore and the Nineteenth of April, 1861,* is a detailed examination of the course of events from February through September 1861. The larger portion of the book deals with the crucial period of April and May 1861 when Maryland's position in the Union remained in doubt. Brown discusses the "midnight ride" of Abraham Lincoln through Baltimore; a passage that did little to endear Lincoln to many Marylanders. The new president, already feared as a "Black Republican," was now held in ridicule by his opponents.

The arrival of the Sixth Massachusetts Volunteer Regiment and the Pennsylvania Militia in Baltimore on April 19, 1861, precipitated one of the most memorable events of the Civil War. Long after countless thousands of skirmishes of the Civil War have been forgotten, the fighting in Baltimore remains the subject of continuing historical interest. An estimated 5,000 Baltimoreans took part in the attacks on Federal troops, which resulted in the deaths of 21 soldiers and civilians and more than 100 injuries. Both sides quickly seized upon the riots to advocate either Maryland's withdrawal from the Union or the need to occupy Baltimore in order to protect the capital city in Washington, D.C. James Ryder Randall's "Maryland, My Maryland" became the rallying cry for pro-Confederate Marylanders—the song is one of the best-known hymns of the Civil War–era.

As we now know, Maryland did not secede from the Union due, in large measure, to the role that George William Brown played during the heady days in the spring of 1861. As such, it is ironic to see how both sides treated Mayor Brown. The Confederacy considered Brown to be one of the martyred Marylanders illegally imprisoned by the tyrannical Lincoln administration. The Federal government, indeed, held Brown for many months without trial. In hindsight, however, Brown's actions as mayor restored order in Baltimore and ensured its occupation by Federal authorities without renewed violence.

Maryland historian J. Thomas Scharf summarized the actions of Baltimore officials on the nineteenth of April:

> It will be seen that during the bloody and memorable occurrences of the 19th of April, the police of Baltimore did all that courage, discipline and subordination to authority could possibly do, to preserve the peace of the city, and protect the troops from violence. Whatever may have been their opinions as to the course of the administration in calling out troops, they were resolute to discharge the duties imposed upon them by the laws of Maryland and they did so faithfully. In the midst of the surging and overwhelming masses, and the scenes of violence and bloodshed that were provoked by the presence of these Northern troops, their conduct was calm, vigilant and resolute, and worthy of praise. Marshal Kane and Deputy Marshal Gifford especially distinguished themselves; while the courageous deportment of Mayor Brown, who marched with them through the furious crowds, risking his life to maintain order, as far as it was possible, and vindicate the authority of the city, was the theme of general praise. It was a perilous and difficult duty fearlessly performed.[9]

By Brown's own account, he was in the thick of the fighting in Baltimore and tried to prevent both soldiers and civilians from committing acts of violence. One Union officer recalled Mayor Brown's presence on the streets "by marching at the head of the column, and remaining there at the risk of his life." In a mass meeting held in Monument Square just hours after the departure of the Northern troops, Mayor Brown denounced the day's disorders and called for the restoration of law and order. Facing an agitated crowd, Brown also decried any efforts to leave the Union. At this same meeting, Governor Thomas Holliday Hicks declared that "I am a Marylander; I love my State and I love the Union, but I will suffer my right

---

[9] Scharf, *History of Maryland,* 3:412–13.

arm to be torn from my body before I will raise it to strike a sister State."

Yet, as fate has it, Governor Hicks is best remembered for delaying his call for the Maryland legislation to meet in Frederick and for the subsequent failure of the House of Delegates to adopt an ordinance of secession. By that point, Federal troops had occupied the state and Maryland's opportunity to join the new Confederacy had vanished. Confederate Marylanders would forever remember Hicks with disdain.[10]

Unlike Baltimore's police marshal, George P. Kane, who later left Baltimore for Virginia and aided Southern efforts to organize the Maryland Line in the Confederate army, Mayor Brown did not support the Southern cause. Instead, Brown was swept up by the Union army as a security threat and held as a prisoner for the remainder of his term as Baltimore's mayor. President Lincoln's suspension of *habeas corpus* on April 27, 1861, followed by Union General Benjamin F. Butler's occupation of Baltimore in mid May, marked both the beginning of Brown's personal tragedy and one of the greatest constitutional crises in American history.

On May 25, Union soldiers under the authority of General George Cadwalader seized John Merryman, a citizen of Maryland, and held him in confinement. Supreme Court Chief Justice Roger Brooks Taney demanded Merryman's release, which precipitated a crisis between the judicial and executive branches of the government. The Lincoln administration, however, essentially ignored the aging Chief Justice's order, although Merryman was let go shortly afterwards. Undeterred

---

[10] See Lawrence M. Denton, *A Southern Star for Maryland: Maryland and the Secession Crisis, 1860–1861* (Baltimore: Concepts Publishers, 1995); and Bart Rhett Talbert, *Maryland: The South's First Casualty* (Berryville: Rockbridge Publishers, 1995).

by legal restraints, the Union army conducted mass arrests of Maryland civilians, including Mayor Brown and a number of Maryland legislators and newspaper editors, in September 1861.

A midnight knock on the door of Brown's country estate roused Brown from bed and he was taken to Fort McHenry in Baltimore. From there, Brown and the other prisoners were transferred to other Northern prisons and eventually arrived at Fort Warren in Boston harbor.[11] Years afterwards, Brown still asked why he had been arrested by Major General John A. Dix, the Federal commander in Baltimore. The months that Brown spent as a prisoner no doubt caused him both physical and spiritual discomfort, yet gave him ample time to reflect on his own situation and that which faced his nation.

In late January 1862, shortly after his return to Fort Warren from a thirty-day parole, Brown wrote his brother-in-law that "this has been a beautiful day. There was a parade of the five companies, with a band of music, and an inspection by Col. [Justin] Dimick. It seemed strange to be under the national flag, and to listen to hail Columbia—not now however happy land—while I was held as a prisoner and regarded as an enemy."[12] The following month, Brown reflected on the Federal government's failure to preserve civil liberties. Writing after major Union successes in the western theater, Brown noted that "I fully appreciate the extent and importance of the Northern victories, but it does not seem to me that the obligation of the administration to respect the Constitution

---

[11] For the signatures of Maryland political prisoners imprisoned with Mayor Brown, see Fort Warren Prisoners' Record Book, Manuscripts Division, Maryland Historical Society, Baltimore, Md.

[12] George W. Brown to George C. Shattuck, January 31, 1862, in George William Brown Papers, MS 2398, Manuscripts Division, Maryland Historical Society.

and the laws is at all diminished by the fact. If they continue to be disregarded, to what end is the country drifting? This is a serious question," Brown added, "and I deal with it, with all the feeling of responsibility which belongs to such a question. After having been severely punished by a long illegal imprisonment for a fault which I never committed, I feel that I am now entitled to the protection which the Constitution promises me."[13]

Perhaps more than anything else, Brown was saddened by the war that tore apart Maryland and the United States. "The more I think of the matter," he wrote in April 1862, "the more do I grieve from the bottom of my soul over the dissolution of the ties political & fraternal which held this people together, and yet sometimes I think looking at the fierce antagonism that had grown up between North & South that the war was inevitable. The sections had got to the point where they must fight it out."[14]

As he described in his book, Brown was adamant that the Federal government release him from prison without his taking the oath of allegiance. To this end, Brown's friends, including noted Baltimore Unionist Enoch Pratt, appealed to Secretary of State William H. Seward for his release. "I understand there was no particular charge against him and as his term has expired & is no longer mayor, I hope he may be unconditionally released & I think this is the sentiment of a large part of our Union men," wrote Pratt from Baltimore in November 1862.[15]

---

[13] Brown to Shattuck, February 21, 1862, Brown Papers, MHS.

[14] Brown to Shattuck, April 11, 1862, Brown Papers, MHS.

[15] Enoch Pratt to William H. Seward, November 12, 1862, in Record Group 94, Records of the Adjutant General's Office, 1780s–1917, Case Files of Investigations by Levi C. Turner and Lafayette C. Baker, 1861–1866, Microfilm Number 797, Roll 3, National Archives and Records Administration, Washington, D.C.

The Union army released Brown on November 27, 1862, and he retired to his country estate of Reverie. Brown's arrest and imprisonment was by no means the only illegal act done by the Federal government; hundreds of other citizens were also held under questionable authority. Following the end of the war, Brown resumed his public life and served as a member of the state's constitutional convention in 1867. Five years later, Brown was elected without opposition as the Chief Justice of the Supreme Bench of Baltimore. He held this post until 1889, and his retirement was marked with great reverence. Four years previously, Brown had run for mayor of Baltimore on the Fusion ticket, but was defeated by Democrat James Hodges.

Brown's long life was marked not only by distinguished public service, but by his many contributions to Maryland's intellectual development. Brown held a number of important civic posts and he was among the founders of the Baltimore Bar Library, the Peabody Institute, and the Maryland Historical Society. He served as a regent to the University of Maryland, a visitor of St. John's College, and as trustee of the Johns Hopkins University, as well as president of the Athenaeum Club. He was a noted lawyer in Baltimore and lectured on constitutional law at the University of Maryland's Law School.

His sudden death from a stroke while vacationing in New York on September 5, 1890, closed a tragic chapter in Maryland's history. George William Brown, born in Baltimore in 1812, just as the United States fought to maintain its independence from Great Britain, witnessed his city's phenomenal rise to national prominence in the nineteenth century. Brown played a leading role in shaping Baltimore's destiny and he recognized the dangers of growing urbanism and unrest. Convinced from an early age that law and order was essential to maintain domestic harmony, Brown democratically seized the reins of power from one of America's most peculiar and violent political parties, the Know-Nothings.

The outbreak of the Civil War completely overshadowed his efforts to bring municipal reform to Baltimore. From his earliest years, Brown was repelled by mob rule and he fought it during the Bank Riots as well as throughout the 1850s. In 1861, Brown found himself confronting near anarchy, this time in the form of an uprising against Federal troops. In his role as mayor, Brown restored order and quelled unrest, thus ensuring a smooth occupation by Union forces. He acted as he would have regardless of the political winds; the rule of law was Brown's guiding hand.

In closing his inaugural address in November 1860, Mayor Brown commented that "surely no cause has yet arisen sufficient to justify the overthrow of the noblest and most beneficial government ever established by human wisdom, and which is consecrated and endeared to the hearts of all, not only by the abundant blessings of the present moment, but by the sacred memories of the past and the great hopes of the future."

Twenty-seven years later, Brown wrote in his *Baltimore and the Nineteenth of April, 1861* that "I believe that the results achieved—namely, the preservation of the Union and the abolition of slavery—are all worth what they have cost." Ever a Unionist and a Marylander, Mayor George William Brown paid a heavy price between 1861 and 1865. His book, *Baltimore and the Nineteenth of April, 1861*, is a poignant reminder of one Marylander's Civil War.

Kevin Conley Ruffner
January 2001

Baltimore and the Nineteenth of April, 1861

CONTENTS.

CHAPTER I.

CHAPTER II.

CHAPTER III.

CHAPTER IV.

Contents.

CHAPTER V.

CHAPTER VI.

CHAPTER VII.

CHAPTER VIII.

Contents.

Contents.

APPENDIX VI.

Baltimore and the Nineteenth of April, 1861

BALTIMORE AND THE NINETEENTH OF APRIL, 1861.

A STUDY OF THE WAR.

CHAPTER I.

INTRODUCTION.—THE FIRST BLOOD SHED IN THE WAR.—THE SUPPOSED PLOT TO ASSASSINATE THE INCOMING PRESIDENT.—THE MIDNIGHT RIDE TO WASHINGTON.

I have often been solicited by persons of widely opposite political opinions to write an account of the events which occurred in Baltimore on the 19th of April, 1861, about which much that is exaggerated and sensational has been circulated; but, for different reasons, I have delayed complying with the request until this time.

These events were not isolated facts, but were the natural result of causes which had roots deep in the past, and they were followed by serious and important consequences. The narrative, to be complete, must give some account of both cause and consequence, and to do this briefly and with a proper regard to historical proportion is no easy task.

Moreover, it is not pleasant to disturb the ashes of a great conflagration, which, although they have grown cold on the surface, cover embers still capable of emitting both smoke and heat; and especially is it not pleasant when the disturber of the ashes was himself an actor in the scenes which he is asked to describe.

But more than twenty-five years have passed, and with them have passed away most of the generation then living; and, as one of the rapidly diminishing survivors, I am admonished by the lengthening shadows that anything I may have to say should be said speedily. The nation has learned many lessons of wisdom from its civil war, and not the least among them is that every truthful contribution to its annals or to its teachings is not without some value.

I have accordingly undertaken the task, but not without reluctance, because it necessarily revives recollections of the most trying and painful experiences of my life—experiences which for a long time I have not unwillingly permitted to fade in the dim distance.

There was another 19th of April—that of Lexington in 1775—which has become memorable in history for a battle between the Minute Men of Massachusetts and a column of British troops, in which the first blood was shed in the war of the Revolution. It was the heroic beginning of that contest.

The fight which occurred in the streets of Baltimore on the 19th of April, 1861, between the 6th Regiment of Massachusetts Volunteers and a mob of citizens, was also memorable, because then was shed the first blood in a conflict between the North and the South; then a step was taken which made compromise or retreat almost impossible; then passions on both sides were aroused which could not be controlled.[1] In each case the outbreak was an explosion of

---

[1] At Fort Sumter, it is true, one week earlier, the first collision of arms had taken place; but strangely, that bombardment was unattended with loss of life. And it did not necessarily mean war between North and South: accommodation still seemed possible.

conflicting forces long suppressed, but certain, sooner or later, to occur. Here the coincidence ends. The Minute Men of Massachusetts were so called because they were prepared to rise on a minute's notice. They had anticipated and had prepared for the strife. The attack by the mob in Baltimore was a sudden uprising of popular fury. The events themselves were magnified as the tidings flashed over the whole country, and the consequences were immediate. The North became wild with astonishment and rage, and the South rose to fever-heat from the conviction that Maryland was about to fall into line as the advance guard of the Southern Confederacy.

In February, 1861, when Mr. Lincoln was on his way to Washington to prepare for his inauguration as President of the United States, an unfortunate incident occurred which had a sinister influence on the State of Maryland, and especially on the city of Baltimore. Some superserviceable persons, carried away, honestly no doubt, by their own frightened imaginations, and perhaps in part stimulated by the temptation of getting up a sensation of the first class, succeeded in persuading Mr. Lincoln that a formidable conspiracy existed to assassinate him on his way through Maryland.

It was announced publicly that he was to come from Philadelphia, not by the usual route through Wilmington, but by a circuitous journey through Harrisburg, and thence by the Northern Central Railroad to Baltimore. Misled by this statement, I, as Mayor of the city, accompanied by the Police Commissioners and supported by a strong force of police, was at the Calvert-street station on Saturday morning, February 23d, at half-past eleven o'clock, the appointed time of arrival, ready to receive with due respect the incoming President. An

open carriage was in waiting, in which I was to have the honor
of escorting Mr. Lincoln through the city to the Washington
station, and of sharing in any danger which he might
encounter.   It is hardly necessary to say that I apprehended
none.   When the train came it appeared, to my great astonishment, that Mrs. Lincoln and her three sons had arrived
safely and without hindrance or molestation of any kind, but
that Mr. Lincoln could not be found.   It was then announced
that he had passed through the city *incognito* in the night
train by the Philadelphia, Wilmington and Baltimore Railroad, and had reached Washington in safety at the usual
hour in the morning.   For this signal deliverance from an
imaginary peril, those who devised the ingenious plan of
escape were of course devoutly thankful, and they accordingly
took to themselves no little amount of credit for its success.

If Mr. Lincoln had arrived in Baltimore at the time
expected, and had spoken a few words to the people who had
gathered to hear him, expressing the kind feelings which
were in his heart with the simple eloquence of which he was
so great a master, he could not have failed to make a very
different impression from that which was produced not only
by the want of confidence and respect manifested towards the
city of Baltimore by the plan pursued, but still more by the
manner in which it was carried out.   On such an occasion
as this even trifles are of importance, and this incident was
not a trifle.   The emotional part of human nature is its
strongest side and soonest leads to action.   It was so with the
people of Baltimore.   Fearful accounts of the conspiracy
flew all over the country, creating a hostile feeling against
the city, from which it soon afterwards suffered.   A single
specimen of the news thus spread will suffice.   A dispatch
from Harrisburg, Pennsylvania, to the New York *Times,*

dated February 23d, 8 A. M., says: "Abraham Lincoln, the President-elect of the United States, is safe in the capital of the nation." Then, after describing the dreadful nature of the conspiracy, it adds: "The list of the names of the conspirators presented a most astonishing array of persons high in Southern confidence, and some whose fame is not confined to this country alone."

Of course, the list of names was never furnished, and all the men in buckram vanished in air. This is all the notice which this matter would require except for the extraordinary narrative contributed by Mr. Samuel M. Felton, at that time President of the Philadelphia, Wilmington and Baltimore Railroad Company, to the volume entitled "A History of Massachusetts in the Civil War," published in 1868.

Early in 1861, Mr. Felton had made, as he supposed, a remarkable discovery of "a deep-laid conspiracy to capture Washington and break up the Government."

Soon afterwards Miss Dix, the philanthropist, opportunely came to his office on a Saturday afternoon, stating that she had an important communication to make to him personally, and then, with closed doors and for more than an hour, she poured into his ears a thrilling tale, to which he attentively listened. "The sum of all was (I quote the language of Mr. Felton) that there was then an extensive and organized conspiracy throughout the South to seize upon Washington, with its archives and records, and then declare the Southern conspirators *de facto* the Government of the United States. The whole was to be a *coup d'état*. At the same time they were to cut off all modes of communication between Washington and the North, East or West, and thus prevent the transportation of troops to wrest the capital from the hands of the insurgents. Mr. Lincoln's inauguration was thus to be prevented, or his life was to fall a sacrifice to the attempt at inauguration. In fact, troops were then drilling on the line of our own road, and the Washington and Annapolis line and other lines."

It was clear that the knowledge of a treasonable conspiracy of such vast proportions, which had already begun its operations, ought not to be confined solely to the keeping of Mr. Felton and Miss Dix. Mr. N. P. Trist, an officer of the road, was accordingly admitted into the secret, and was dispatched in haste to Washington, to lay all the facts before General Scott, the Commander-in-Chief. The General, however, would give no assurances except that he would do all he could to bring sufficient troops to Washington to make it secure. Matters stood in this unsatisfactory condition for some time, until a new rumor reached the ears of Mr. Felton.

A gentleman from Baltimore, he says, came out to Back River Bridge, about five miles east of the city, and told the bridgekeeper that he had information which had come to his knowledge, of vital importance to the road, which he wished communicated to Mr. Felton. The nature of this communication was that a party was then organized in Baltimore to burn the bridges in case Mr. Lincoln came over the road, or in case an attempt was made to carry troops for the defense of Washington. The party at that time had combustible materials prepared to pour over the bridges, and were to disguise themselves as negroes and be at the bridge just before the train in which Mr. Lincoln travelled had arrived. The bridge was then to be burned, the train attacked, and Mr. Lincoln to be put out of the way. The man appeared several times, always, it seems, to the bridgekeeper, and he always communicated new information about the conspirators, but he would never give his name nor place of abode, and both still remain a mystery. Mr. Felton himself then went to Washington, where he succeeded in obtaining from a prominent gentleman from Baltimore whom he there saw, the judicious advice to apply to Marshal Kane, the Chief of Police in Baltimore, with the assurance that he was a perfectly reliable person. Marshal Kane was accordingly seen, but he scouted the idea that there was any such thing on foot as a conspiracy to burn the bridges and cut off Washington, and said he had thoroughly investigated the whole matter, and there was not the slightest foundation for such rumors. Mr. Felton was not satisfied, but he would have nothing more to do with Marshal Kane. He next sent for a celebrated detective in the West, whose name is not given, and through this chief and his subordinates every nook and corner of the road and its vicinity was explored. They reported that they had joined the societies of the conspirators in Baltimore and got into their secrets, and that the secret working of secession and treason was laid bare, with all its midnight plottings and daily consultations. The conspiracy being thus proved to Mr. Felton's satisfaction, he at once organized and armed a force of two hundred men and scattered them along the line of the railroad between the Susquehanna and Baltimore, principally at the bridges. But, strange to say, all that was accomplished by this formidable body was an enormous job of whitewashing.

The narrative proceeds: " These men were drilled secretly and regularly by drill-masters, and were apparently employed in whitewashing the bridges, putting on some six or seven coats of whitewash saturated with salt and alum, to make the outside of the bridges as nearly fireproof as possible. This whitewashing, so extensive in its application, became (continues Mr. Felton) the nine days' wonder of the neighborhood." And well it might. After the lapse of twenty-five years the wonder over this feat of strategy can hardly yet have ceased in that rural and peaceful neighborhood. But, unfortunately for Mr. Felton's peace of mind, the programme of Mr. Lincoln's journey was suddenly changed. He had selected a different route. He had decided to go to Harrisburg from Philadelphia, and thence by day to Baltimore, over another and a rival road, known as the Northern Central. Then the chief detective discovered that the attention of the conspirators was suddenly turned to the Northern Central road. The mysterious unknown gentleman from Baltimore appeared again on the scene and confirmed this statement. He gave warning that Mr. Lincoln was to be waylaid and his life sacrificed on that road, on which no whitewash had been used, and where there were no armed men to protect him.

Mr. Felton hurried to Philadelphia, and there, in a hotel, joined his chief detective, who was registered under a feigned name. Mr. Lincoln, cheered by a dense crowd, was, at that moment, passing through the streets of Philadelphia. A sub-detective was sent to bring Mr. Judd, Mr. Lincoln's intimate friend, to the hotel to hold a consultation. Mr. Judd was in the procession with Mr. Lincoln, but the emergency admitted no delay. The eagerness of the sub-detective was so great that he was three times arrested and carried out of the crowd by the police before he could reach Mr. Judd. The fourth attempt succeeded, and Mr. Judd was at last brought to the hotel, where he met both Mr. Felton and the chief detective. The narrative then proceeds in the words of Mr. Felton: "We lost no time in making known to him (Mr. Judd) all the facts which had come to our knowledge in reference to the conspiracy, and I most earnestly advised that Mr. Lincoln should go to Washington privately in the sleeping-car. Mr. Judd fully entered into the plan, and said he would urge Mr. Lincoln to adopt it. On his communicating with Mr. Lincoln, after the services of the evening were over, he answered that he had engaged to go to Harrisburg and speak the next day, and that he would not break his engagement, even in the face of such peril, but that after he had fulfilled his engagement he would follow such advice as we might give him in reference to his journey to Washington." Mr. Lincoln accordingly went to Harrisburg the next day and made an address. After that the arrangements for the journey were shrouded in the profoundest mystery. It was given out that he was to go to Governor Curtin's house for the night, but he was, instead, conducted to a point about two miles out of Harrisburg, where an extra car and engine waited to take him to Philadelphia. The telegraph lines east, west, north and south from Harrisburg were cut, so that no message as to his movements could be sent off in any direction. But all this caused a detention, and the night train from Philadelphia to Baltimore had to be held back until the arrival of Mr. Lincoln at the former place. If, however, the delay proved to be considerable, when Mr. Lincoln reached Baltimore the connecting train to Washington might leave without him. But Mr. Felton was equal to the occasion. He devised a plan which was communicated to only three or four on the road. A messenger was sent to Baltimore by an earlier train to say to the officials of the Washington road that a very important package must be delivered in Washington early in the morning, and to request them to wait for the night train from Philadelphia. To give color to this statement, a package of old railroad reports, done up with great care, and with a large seal attached, marked by Mr. Felton's own hand, " Very Important," was sent in the train which carried Mr. Lincoln on his famous night ride from Philadelphia through Maryland and Baltimore to the city of Washington. The only remarkable incident of the journey was the mysterious behavior of the few officials who were entrusted with the portentous secret.

I do not know how others may be affected by this narrative, but I confess even now to a feeling of indignation that Mr. Lincoln, who was no coward, but proved himself on many an occasion to be a brave man, was thus prevented from carrying out his original intention of journeying to Baltimore in the light of day, in company with his wife and children, relying as he always did on the honor and manhood of the American people. It is true we have, to our sorrow, learned by the manner of his death, as well as by the fate of still another President, that no one occupying so high a place can be absolutely safe, even in this country, from the danger of assassination, but it is still true that as a rule the best way to meet such danger is boldly to defy it.

Mr. C. C. Felton, son of Mr. Samuel M. Felton, in an article entitled " The Baltimore Plot," published in December, 1885, in the *Harvard Monthly*, has attempted to revive this absurd story. He repeats the account of whitewashing the bridges, and of the astonishment created among the good people of the neighborhood. He has faith in " the unknown Baltimorean " who visited the bridgekeeper, but would never give his name, and in the spies employed, who, he tells us, were " the well-known detective Pinkerton and eight assistants," and he leaves his readers to infer that Mr. Lincoln's life was saved by the extraordinary vigilance which had been exercised and the ingenious plan which had been devised by his worthy father, but alas!—

" The earth hath bubbles as the water has,"

and this was of them.

Colonel Lamon, a close friend of President Lincoln, and the only person who accompanied him on his night ride to Washington, has written his biography, a very careful and conscientious work, which unfortunately was left unfinished, and he of course had the strongest reasons for carefully examining the subject. After a full examination of all the documents, Colonel Lamon pronounces the conspiracy to be a mere fiction, and adds in confirmation the mature opinion of Mr. Lincoln himself.

Colonel Lamon says:[1] "Mr. Lincoln soon learned to regret the midnight ride. His friends reproached him, his enemies taunted him. He was convinced that he had committed a grave mistake in yielding to the solicitations of a professional spy and of friends too easily alarmed. He saw that he had fled from a danger purely imaginary, and felt the shame and mortification natural to a brave man under such circumstances. But he was not disposed to take all the responsibility to himself, and frequently upbraided the writer for having aided and assisted him to demean himself at the very moment in all his life when his behavior should have exhibited the utmost dignity and composure."

As Colonel Lamon's biography, a work of absorbing interest, is now out of print, and as his account of the ride and of the results of the investigation of the conspiracy is too long to be inserted here, it is added in an Appendix.

The account above given has its appropriateness here, for the midnight ride through Baltimore, and the charge that its citizens were plotting the President's assassination, helped to feed the flame of excitement which, in the stirring events of that time, was already burning too high all over the land, and especially in a border city with divided sympathies.

---

[1] The Life of Abraham Lincoln, p. 526; and see Appendix I.

CHAPTER II.

THE COMPROMISES OF THE CONSTITUTION IN REGARD TO SLAVERY.—A DIVIDED HOUSE.—THE BROKEN COMPACT.— THE RIGHT OF REVOLUTION.

For a period the broad provisions of the Constitution of the United States, as expounded by the wise and broad decisions of the Supreme Court, had proved to be equal to every emergency. The thirteen feeble colonies had grown to be a great Republic, and no external obstacle threatened its majestic progress; foreign wars had been waged and vast territories had been annexed, but every strain on the Constitution only served to make it stronger. Yet there was a canker in a vital part which nothing could heal, which from day to day became more malignant, and which those who looked beneath the surface could perceive was surely leading, and at no distant day, to dissolution or war, or perhaps to both. The canker was the existence of negro slavery.

In colonial days, kings, lords spiritual and temporal, and commons, all united in favoring the slave trade. In Massachusetts the Puritan minister might be seen on the Sabbath going to meeting in family procession, with his negro slave bringing up the rear. Boston was largely engaged in building ships and manufacturing rum, and a portion of the ships and much of the rum were sent to Africa, the rum to buy slaves, and the ships to bring them to a market in America. Newport was more largely, and until a more recent time, engaged in the same traffic.

In Maryland, even the Friends were sometimes owners of

slaves; and it is charged, and apparently with reason, that Wenlock Christison, the Quaker preacher, after being driven from Massachusetts by persecution and coming to Maryland by way of Barbadoes, sent or brought in with him a number of slaves, who cultivated his plantation until his death. In Georgia, the Calvinist Whitefield blessed God for his negro plantation, which was generously given to him to establish his " Bethesda " as a refuge for orphan children.

In the Dred Scott case, Chief Justice Taney truly described the opinion, which he deplored, prevailing at the time of the adoption of the Constitution, as being that the colored man had no rights which the white man was bound to respect.[1]

The Constitution had endeavored to settle the question of slavery by a compromise. As the difficulty in regard to it arose far more from political than moral grounds, so in the settlement the former were almost exclusively considered. It was, however, the best that could be made at that time. It is certain that without such a compromise the Constitution would not have been adopted. The existence of slavery in a State was left in the discretion of the State itself. If a slave escaped to another State, he was to be returned to his master. Laws were passed by Congress to carry out this provision, and the Supreme Court decided that they were constitutional.

For a long time the best people at the North stood firmly by the compromise. It was a national compact, and must be respected. But ideas, and especially moral ideas, cannot be forever fettered by a compact, no matter how solemn may be its sanctions. The change of opinion at the North was first slow, then rapid, and then so powerful as to overwhelm all opposition. John Brown, who was executed for raising a

---

[1] Judge Taney's utterance on this subject has been frequently and grossly misrepresented. In Appendix II. will be found what he really did say.

negro insurrection in Virginia, in which men were wounded and killed, was reverenced by many at the North as a hero, a martyr and a saint. It had long been a fixed fact that no fugitive slave could by process of law be returned from the North into slavery. With the advent to power of the Republican party—a party based on opposition to slavery—another breach in the outworks of the Constitution, as interpreted by the Supreme Court, had been made. Sooner or later the same hands would capture the citadel. Sooner or later it was plain that slavery was doomed.

In the memorable Senatorial campaign in Illinois between Stephen A. Douglas and Abraham Lincoln, the latter, in his speech before the Republican State Convention at Springfield, June 17, 1858, struck the keynote of his party by the bold declaration on the subject of slavery which he then made and never recalled.

This utterance was the more remarkable because on the previous day the convention had passed unanimously a resolution declaring that Mr. Lincoln was their first and only choice for United States Senator, to fill the vacancy about to be created by the expiration of Mr. Douglas's term of office, but the convention had done nothing which called for the advanced ground on which Mr. Lincoln planted himself in that speech. It was carefully prepared.

The narrative of Colonel Lamon in his biography of Lincoln is intensely interesting and dramatic.[1]

About a dozen gentlemen, he says, were called to meet in the library of the State House. After seating them at the round table, Mr. Lincoln read his entire speech, dwelling slowly on that part which speaks of a divided house, so that every man fully understood it. After he had finished, he

---

[1] Lamon's Life of Lincoln, p. 398.

asked for the opinion of his friends. All but William H. Herndon, the law partner of Mr. Lincoln, declared that the whole speech was too far in advance of the times, and they especially condemned that part which referred to a divided house. Mr. Herndon sat still while they were giving their respective opinions; then he sprang to his feet and said: "Lincoln, deliver it just as it reads. If it is in advance of the times, let us—you and I, if no one else—lift the people to the level of this speech now, higher hereafter. The speech is true, wise and politic, and will succeed now, or in the future. Nay, it will aid you, if it will not make you President of the United States." . . . .

"Mr. Lincoln sat still a short moment, rose from his chair, walked backward and forward in the hall, stopped and said: 'Friends, I have thought about this matter a great deal, have weighed the question well from all corners, and am thoroughly convinced the time has come when it should be uttered; and if it must be that I must go down because of this speech, then let me go down linked to truth—die in the advocacy of what is right and just. This nation cannot live on injustice. A house divided against itself cannot stand, I say again and again.'"

The opening paragraph of the speech is as follows: "If we could first know where we are and whither we are tending, we could then better judge what to do and how to do it. We are now far on into the fifth year since a policy was initiated with the avowed object and confident promise of putting an end to slavery agitation. Under the operation of that policy that agitation has not only not ceased, but is constantly augmented. In my opinion, it will not cease until a crisis shall have been reached and passed. A house divided against itself cannot stand. I believe this Government cannot endure permanently half slave and half free. I do not expect the Union to be dissolved. I do not expect the house to fall; but I do expect it will cease to be divided. It will become all one thing, or all the other. Either the opponents of slavery will arrest the further spread of it, and place it where the public mind shall rest in the belief that it is in the course of ultimate extinction, or its advocates will push it forward till it shall become alike lawful in all the States, old as well as new, North as well as South."

The blast of the trumpet gave no uncertain sound. The far-seeing suggestion of Mr. Herndon came true to the letter. I believe this speech made Abraham Lincoln President of the United States.

But the founders of the Constitution of the United States had built a house which was divided against itself from the beginning. They had framed a union of States which was part free and part slave, and that union was intended to last forever. Here was an irreconcilable conflict between the Constitution and the future President of the United States.

When the Republican Convention assembled at Chicago in May, 1860, in the heat of the contest, which soon became narrowed down to a choice between Mr. Seward and Mr. Lincoln, the latter dispatched a friend to Chicago with a message in writing, which was handed either to Judge Davis or Judge Logan, both members of the convention, which runs as follows: " Lincoln agrees with Seward in his irrepressible-conflict idea, and in negro equality; but he is opposed to Seward's higher law." But there was no substantial difference between the position of the two: Lincoln's " divided house" and Seward's "higher law " placed them really in the same attitude.

The seventh resolution in the Chicago platform condemned

what it described as the "new dogma that the Constitution, of its own force, carries slavery into any or all of the Territories of the United States." This resolution was a direct repudiation by a National Convention of the decision of the Supreme Court in the Dred Scott case.

On the 6th of November, 1860, Abraham Lincoln was elected President of the United States. Of the actual votes cast there was a majority against him of 930,170. Next came Mr. Douglas, who lost the support of the Southern Democrats by his advocacy of the doctrine of "squatter sovereignty," as it was called, which was in effect, although not in form, as hostile to the decision of the Supreme Court in the Dred Scott case as the seventh resolution of the Chicago Convention itself. Mr. Breckinridge, of Kentucky, the candidate of the Southern Democracy, fell very far, and Mr. Bell, of Tennessee, the candidate of the Union party, as it was called, a short-lived successor of the old Whig party, fell still farther in the rear of the two Northern candidates.

The great crisis had come at last. The Abolition party had become a portion of the victorious Republican party. The South, politically, was overwhelmed. Separated now from its only ally, the Northern Democracy, it stood at last alone.

It matters not that Mr. Lincoln, after his election, in sincerity of heart held out the olive branch to the nation, and that during his term of office the South, so far as his influence could avail, would have been comparatively safe from direct aggressions. Mr. Lincoln was not known then as he is known now, and, moreover, his term of office would be but four years.

What course, then, was left to the South if it was determined to maintain its rights under the Constitution? What but the right of self-defense?

The house of every man is his castle, and he may defend it to the death against all aggressors. When a hostile hand is raised to strike a blow, he who is assaulted need not wait until the blow falls, but on the instant may protect himself as best he can. These are the rights of self-defense known, approved and acted on by all freemen. And where constitutional rights of a people are in jeopardy, a kindred right of self-defense belongs to them. Although revolutionary in its character, it is not the less a right.

Wendell Phillips, abolitionist as he was, in a speech made at New Bedford on the 9th of April, 1861, three days before the bombardment of Fort Sumter, fully recognized this right. He said: " Here are a series of States girding the Gulf, who think that their peculiar institutions require that they should have a separate government. They have a right to decide that question without appealing to you or me. A large body of the people, sufficient to make a nation, have come to the conclusion that they will have a government of a certain form. Who denies them the right? Standing with the principles of '76 behind us, who can deny them the right? What is a matter of a few millions of dollars or a few forts? It is a mere drop in the bucket of the great national question. It is theirs just as much as ours. I maintain, on the principles of '76, that Abraham Lincoln has no right to a soldier in Fort Sumter."

And such was the honest belief of the people who united in establishing the Southern Confederacy.

Wendell Phillips was not wrong in declaring the principles of '76 to be kindred to those of '61. The men of '76 did not fight to get rid of the petty tax of three pence a pound on tea, which was the only tax left to quarrel about. They were determined to pay no taxes, large or small, then or thereafter. Whether the tax was lawful or not was a doubtful question, about which there was a wide difference of opinion, but they did not care for that. Nothing would satisfy them but the relinquishment of any claim of right to tax the colonies, and this they could not obtain. They maintained that their rights were violated. They were, moreover, embittered by a long series of disputes with the mother country, and they wanted to be independent and to have a country of their own. They thought they were strong enough to maintain that position.

Neither were the Southern men of '61 fighting for money. And they too were deeply embittered, not against a mother country, but against a brother country. The Northern people had published invectives of the most exasperating character broadcast against the South in their speeches, sermons, newspapers and books. The abolitionists had proceeded from words to deeds and were unwearied in tampering with the slaves and carrying them off. The Southern people, on their part, were not less violent in denunciation of the North. The slavery question had divided the political parties throughout the nation, and on this question the South was practically a unit. They could get no security that the provisions of the Constitution would be kept either in letter or in spirit, and this they demanded as their right.

The Southern men thought that they also were strong enough to wage successfully a defensive war. Like the men of '76, they in great part were of British stock ; they lived in a thinly settled country, led simple lives, were accustomed to the use of arms, and knew how to protect themselves. Such men make good soldiers, and when their armies were enrolled the ranks were filled with men of all classes, the rich as well as the poor, the educated as well as the ignorant.

It is a mistake to suppose that they were inveigled into secession by ambitious leaders. On the contrary, it is probable that they were not as much under the influence of leaders as the men of '76, and that there were fewer disaffected among them. At times the scales trembled in the balance. There are always mistakes in war. It is an easy and ungrateful task to point them out afterward. We can now see that grave errors, both financial and military, were made, and that opportunities were thrown away. How far these went to settle the contest, we can never certainly know, but it does not need great boldness to assert that the belief which the Southern people entertained that they were strong enough to defend themselves, was not unreasonable.

The determination of the South to maintain slavery was undoubtedly the main cause of secession, but another deep and underlying cause was the firm belief of the Southern people in the doctrine of States' rights, and their jealousy of any attack upon those rights. Devotion to their State first of all, a conviction that paramount obligation — in case of any conflict of allegiance — was due not to the Union but to the State, had been part of the political creed of very many in the South ever since the adoption of the Constitution. An ignoble love of slavery was not the general and impelling motive. The slaveholders, who were largely in the minority, acted as a privileged class always does act. They were determined to maintain their privileges at all hazards. But they, as well as the great mass of the people who had no personal interest in slavery, fought the battles of the war with the passionate earnestness of men who believed with an undoubting conviction that they were the defenders not only of home rule and of their firesides, but also of their constitutional rights.

And behind the money question, the constitutional question and the moral question, there was still another of the gravest import. Was it possible for two races nearly equal in number, but widely different in character and civilization, to live together in a republic in peace and equality of rights without mingling in blood? The answer of the Southern man was, " It is not possible."

CHAPTER III.

MARYLAND'S DESIRE FOR PEACE.—EVENTS WHICH FOL-
LOWED THE ELECTION OF PRESIDENT LINCOLN.—HIS
PROCLAMATION CALLING FOR TROOPS. — THE CITY
AUTHORITIES AND POLICE OF BALTIMORE.—INCREASING
EXCITEMENT IN BALTIMORE.

I now come to consider the condition of affairs in Maryland. As yet the Republican party had obtained a very slight
foothold. Only 2,294 votes had in the whole State been cast
for Mr. Lincoln. Her sympathies were divided between the
North and the South, with a decided preponderance on the
Southern side. For many years her conscience had been
neither dead nor asleep on the subject of slavery. Families
had impoverished themselves to free their slaves. In 1860
there were 83,942 free colored people in Maryland and 87,189
slaves, the white population being 515,918. Thus there
were nearly as many free as slaves of the colored race.
Emancipation, in spite of harsh laws passed to discounte-
nance it, had rapidly gone on. In the northern part of the
State and in the city of Baltimore there were but few slaveholders, and the slavery was hardly more than nominal. The
patriarchal institution, as it has been derisively called, had a
real existence in many a household. Not a few excellent
people have I known and respected who were born and bred
in slavery and had been freed by their masters. In 1831 the
State incorporated the Maryland Colonization Society, which
founded on the west coast of Africa a successful republican
colony of colored people, now known as the State of Maryland

in Liberia, and for twenty-six years, and until the war broke out, the State contributed $10,000 a year to its support. This amount was increased by the contributions of individuals. The board, of which Mr. John H. B. Latrobe was for many years president, was composed of our best citizens. A code of laws for the government of the colony was prepared by the excellent and learned lawyer, Hugh Davey Evans.

While there was on the part of a large portion of the people a deep-rooted and growing dislike to slavery, agitation on the subject had not commenced. It was in fact suppressed by reason of the violence of Northern abolitionists with whom the friends of emancipation were not able to unite.

It is not surprising that Maryland was in no mood for war, but that her voice was for compromise and peace—compromise and peace at any price consistent with honor.

The period immediately following the election of Mr. Lincoln in November, 1860, was throughout the country one of intense agitation and of important events. A large party at the North preferred compromise to war, even at the cost of dissolution of the Union. If dissolution began, no one could tell where it would stop. South Carolina seceded on the 17th of December, 1860. Georgia and the five Gulf States soon followed. On the 6th of January, 1861, Fernando Wood, mayor of the city of New York, sent a message to the common council advising that New York should secede and become a free city.[1]

---

[1] John P. Kennedy, of Baltimore, the well-known author, who had been member of Congress and Secretary of the Navy, published early in 1861 a pamphlet entitled "The Border States, Their Power and Duty in the Present Disordered Condition of the Country." His idea was that if concert of action could be had between the Border States and concurring States of the South which had not seceded, stipulations might be obtained from the Free States, with the aid of Congress, and, if necessary, an amendment of

On February the 9th, Jefferson Davis was elected President of the Southern Confederacy, a Confederacy to which other States would perhaps soon be added. But the Border States were as yet debatable ground; they might be retained by conciliation and compromise or alienated by hostile measures, whether directed against them or against the seceded States. In Virginia a convention had been called to consider the momentous question of union or secession, and an overwhelming majority of the delegates chosen were in favor of remaining in the Union. Other States were watching Virginia's course, in order to decide whether to stay in the Union or go out of it with her.

On the 12th and 13th of April occurred the memorable bombardment and surrender of Fort Sumter. On the 15th of April, President Lincoln issued his celebrated proclamation calling out seventy-five thousand militia, and appealing "to all loyal citizens to favor, facilitate and aid this effort to maintain the honor, the integrity and existence of our National Union, and the perpetuity of popular government, and to redress wrongs already long enough endured." What

---

the Constitution, which would protect the rights of the South; but if this failed, that the Border States and their allies of the South would then be forced to consider the Union impracticable and to organize a separate confederacy of the Border States, with the association of such of the Southern and Free States as might be willing to accede to the proposed conditions. He hoped that the Union would thus be "reconstructed by the healthy action of the Border States." The necessary result, however, would have been that in the meantime three confederacies would have been in existence. And yet Mr. Kennedy had always been a Union man, and when the war broke out was its consistent advocate.

These proposals, from such different sources as Fernando Wood and John P. Kennedy, tend to show the uncertainty and bewilderment which had taken possession of the minds of men, and in which few did not share to a greater or less degree.

these wrongs were is not stated. "The first service assigned to the forces hereby called forth," said the proclamation, "will probably be to re-possess the forts, places and property which have been seized from the Union." On the same day there was issued from the War Department a request addressed to the Governors of the different States, announcing what the quota of each State would be, and that the troops were to serve for three months unless sooner discharged. Maryland's quota was four regiments.

The proclamation was received with exultation at the North—many dissentient voices being silenced in the general acclaim—with defiance at the South, and in Maryland with mingled feelings in which astonishment, dismay and disapprobation were predominant. On all sides it was agreed that the result must be war, or a dissolution of the Union, and I may safely say that a large majority of our people then preferred the latter.

An immediate effect of the proclamation was to intensify the feeling of hostility in the wavering States, and to drive four of them into secession. Virginia acted promptly. On April 17th her convention passed an ordinance of secession—subject to ratification by a vote of the people—and Virginia became the head and front of the Confederacy. North Carolina, Tennessee and Arkansas soon followed her lead. Meanwhile, and before the formal acts of secession, the Governors of Virginia, North Carolina and Tennessee sent prompt and defiant answers to the requisition, emphatically refusing to furnish troops, as did also the Governors of Kentucky and Missouri.

The position of Maryland was most critical. This State was especially important, because the capital of the nation lay within her borders, and all the roads from the North leading to it passed through her territory. After the President's proclamation was issued, no doubt a large majority of her people sympathized with the South; but even had that sentiment been far more preponderating, there was an underlying feeling that by a sort of geographical necessity her lot was cast with the North, that the larger and stronger half of the nation would not allow its capital to be quietly disintegrated away by her secession. Delaware and Maryland were the only Border States which did not attempt to secede. Kentucky at first took the impossible stand of an armed neutrality. When this failed, a portion of her people passed an ordinance of secession, and a portion of the people of Missouri passed a similar ordinance.

It is now proper to give some explanation of the condition of affairs in Baltimore, at that time a city of 215,000 inhabitants.

Thomas Holliday Hicks, who had been elected by the American, or Know-Nothing party, three years before, was the Governor of the State. The city authorities, consisting of the mayor and city council, had been elected in October, 1860, a few weeks before the Presidential election, not as representatives of any of the national parties, but as the candidates of an independent reform party, and in opposition to the Know-Nothing party. This party, which then received its quietus, had been in power for some years, and had maintained itself by methods which made its rule little better than a reign of terror.[1] No one acquainted with the history of that

---

[1] The culmination of this period of misrule was at the election in November, 1859, when the fraud and violence were so flagrant that the Legislature of the State unseated the whole Baltimore delegation—ten members. The city being thus without representation, it became necessary, when a special session of the Legislature was called in April, 1861, that a new delegation

period can doubt that the reform was greatly needed. A large number of the best men of the American party united in the movement, and with their aid it became triumphantly successful, carrying every ward in the city. The city council was composed of men of unusually high character. " Taken as a whole" (Scharf's " History of Maryland," Vol. III., p. 284), "a better ticket has seldom, if ever, been brought out. In the selection of candidates all party tests were discarded, and all thought of rewarding partisan services repudiated." Four police commissioners, appointed by the Legislature—Charles Howard, William H. Gatchell, Charles D. Hinks and John W. Davis—men of marked ability and worth, had, with the mayor, who was *ex officio* a member of the board, the appointment and control of the police force. Mr. S. Teackle Wallis was the legal adviser of the board. The entire police force consisted of 398 men, and had been raised to a high degree of discipline and efficiency under the command of Marshal Kane. They were armed with revolvers.

Immediately after the call of the President for troops, including four regiments from Maryland, a marked division among the people manifested itself. Two large and excited crowds, eager for news, and nearly touching each other, stood from morning until late at night before two newspaper offices on Baltimore street which advocated contrary views and opinions. Strife was in the air. It was difficult for the police to keep the peace. Business was almost suspended. Was there indeed to be war between the sections, or could it yet, by some

---

from Baltimore should be chosen. It was this same Legislature (elected in 1859) which took away from the mayor of the city the control of its police, and entrusted that force to a board of police commissioners. This change, a most fortunate one for the city at that crisis, resulted in the immediate establishment of good order, and made possible the reform movement of the next autumn.

unlooked-for interposition, be averted? Would the Border
States interfere and demand peace? There was a deep and
pervading impression of impending evil. And now an immediate fear was as to the effect on the citizens of the passage of
Northern troops through the city. Should they be permitted
to cross the soil of Maryland, to make war on sister States of
the South, allied to her by so many ties of affection, as well
as of kindred institutions? On the other hand, when the
capital of the nation was in danger, should not the kindest
greeting and welcome be extended to those who were first to
come to the rescue? Widely different were the answers given
to these questions. The Palmetto flag had several times been
raised by some audacious hands in street and harbor, but it
was soon torn down. The National flag and the flag of the
State, with its black and orange, the colors of Lord Baltimore,
waved unmolested, but not side by side, for they had become
symbols of different ideas, although the difference was, as yet,
not clearly defined.

On the 17th of April, the state of affairs became so serious
that I, as mayor, issued a proclamation earnestly invoking all
good citizens to refrain from every act which could lead to
outbreak or violence of any kind; to refrain from harshness
of speech, and to render in all cases prompt and efficient aid,
as by law they were required to do, to the public authorities,
whose constant efforts would be exerted to maintain unbroken
the peace and order of the city, and to administer the laws
with fidelity and impartiality. I cannot flatter myself that
this appeal produced much effect. The excitement was too
great for any words to allay it.

On the 18th of April, notice was received from Harrisburg
that two companies of United States artillery, commanded by
Major Pemberton, and also four companies of militia, would

arrive by the Northern Central Railroad at Bolton Station, in the northern part of the city, at two o'clock in the afternoon. The militia had neither arms nor uniforms.

Before the troops arrived at the station, where I was waiting to receive them, I was suddenly called away by a message from Governor Hicks stating that he desired to see me on business of urgent importance, and this prevented my having personal knowledge of what immediately afterward occurred. The facts, however, are that a large crowd assembled at the station and followed the soldiers in their march to the Washington station with abuse and threats. The regulars were not molested, but the wrath of the mob was directed against the militia, and an attack would certainly have been made but for the vigilance and determination of the police, under the command of Marshal Kane.

"These proceedings," says Mr. Scharf, in the third volume of his "History of Maryland," page 401, "were an earnest of what might be expected on the arrival of other troops, the excitement growing in intensity with every hour. Numerous outbreaks occurred in the neighborhood of the newspaper offices during the day, and in the evening a meeting of the States Rights Convention was held in Taylor's building, on Fayette street near Calvert, where, it is alleged, very strong ground was taken against the passage of any more troops through Baltimore, and armed resistance to it threatened. On motion of Mr. Ross Winans, the following resolutions were unanimously adopted:

" *Resolved*, That in the opinion of this convention the prosecution of the design announced by the President in his late proclamation, of recapturing the forts in the seceded States, will inevitably lead to a sanguinary war, the dissolution of the Union, and the irreconcilable estrangement of the people of the South from the people of the North.

" *Resolved*, That we protest in the name of the people of Maryland against the garrisoning of Southern forts by militia drawn from the free States; or the quartering of militia from the free States in any of the towns or places of the slaveholding States.

"*Resolved,* That in the opinion of this convention the massing of large bodies of militia, exclusively from the free States, in the District of Columbia, is uncalled for by any public danger or exigency, is a standing menace to the State of Maryland, and an insult to her loyalty and good faith, and will, if persisted in, alienate her people from a government which thus attempts to overawe them by the presence of armed men and treats them with contempt and distrust.

"*Resolved,* That the time has arrived when it becomes all good citizens to unite in a common effort to obliterate all party lines which have heretofore unhappily divided us, and to present an unbroken front in the preservation and defense of our interests, our homes and our firesides, to avert the horrors of civil war, and to repel, if need be, any invader who may come to establish a military despotism over us.

"A. C. ROBINSON, Chairman."

"G. HARLAN WILLIAMS,
"ALBERT RITCHIE,
        "*Secretaries.*"

The names of the members who composed this convention are not given, but the mover of the resolutions and the officers of the meeting were men well known and respected in this community.

The bold and threatening character of the resolutions did not tend to calm the public mind. They did not, however, advocate an attack on the troops.

In Putnam's "Record of the Rebellion," Volume I, page 29, the following statement is made of a meeting which was held on the morning of the 18th of April: "An excited secession meeting was held at Baltimore, Maryland. T. Parkin Scott occupied the chair, and speeches denunciatory of the Administration and the North were made by Wilson C. N. Carr, William Byrne [improperly spelled Burns], President of the National Volunteer Association, and others."

An account of the meeting is before me, written by Mr. Carr, lately deceased, a gentleman entirely trustworthy. He did not know, he says, of the existence of such an association, but on his way down town having seen the notice of a town meeting to be held at Taylor's Hall, to take into consideration the state of affairs, he went to the meeting. Mr. Scott was in the chair and was speaking. He was not making an excited speech, but, on the contrary, was urging the audience to do nothing rashly, but to be moderate and not to interfere with any troops that might attempt to pass through the city. As soon as he had finished, Mr. Carr was urged to go up to the platform and reply to Mr. Scott. I now give Mr. Carr's words. "I went up," he says, "but had no intention of saying anything in opposition to what Mr. Scott had advised the people to do. I was not there as an advocate of secession, but was anxious to see some way opened for reconciliation between the North and South. I did not make an excited speech nor did I denounce the Administration. I saw that I was disappointing the crowd. Some expressed their disapprobation pretty plainly and I cut my speech short. As soon as I finished speaking the meeting adjourned."

After the war was over, Mr. Scott was elected Chief Judge of the Supreme Bench of Baltimore City. He was a strong sympathizer with the South, and had the courage of his convictions, but he had been also an opponent of slavery, and I have it from his own lips that years before the war, on a Fourth of July, he had persuaded his mother to liberate all her slaves, although she depended largely on their services for her support. And yet he lived and died a poor man.

On the 16th of April, Marshal Kane addressed a letter to William Crawford, the Baltimore agent of the Philadelphia, Wilmington and Baltimore Railroad Company, in the following terms:

"*Dear Sir :*—Is it true as stated that an attempt will be made to pass the volunteers from New York intended to war upon the South over your road to-day? It is important that we have explicit understanding on the subject.   Your friend,   GEORGE P. KANE."

This letter was not submitted to me, nor to the board of police. If it had been, it would have been couched in very different language. Mr. Crawford forwarded it to the President of the road, who, on the same day, sent it to Simon Cameron, the Secretary of War.

Mr. Cameron, on April 18th, wrote to Governor Hicks, giving him notice that there were unlawful combinations of citizens of Maryland to impede the transit of United States troops across Maryland on their way to the defense of the capital, and that the President thought it his duty to make it known to the Governor, so that all loyal and patriotic citizens might be warned in time, and that he might be prepared to take immediate and effective measures against it.

On the afternoon of the 18th, Governor Hicks arrived in town. He had prepared a proclamation as Governor of the State, and wished me to issue another as mayor of the city, which I agreed to do. In it he said, among other things, that the unfortunate state of affairs now existing in the country had greatly excited the people of Maryland; that the emergency was great, and that the consequences of a rash step would be fearful. He therefore counselled the people in all earnestness to withhold their hands from whatever might tend to precipitate us into the gulf of discord and ruin gaping to receive us. All powers vested in the Governor of the State would be strenuously exerted to preserve peace and maintain inviolate the honor and integrity of Maryland. He assured the people that no troops would be sent from Maryland, unless it might be for the defense of the national capital. He concluded by saying that the people of this State would in a short time have the opportunity afforded them, in a special election for members of Congress, to express their devotion to the Union, or their desire to see it broken up.

This proclamation is of importance in several respects. It shows the great excitement of the people and the imminent danger of domestic strife. It shows, moreover, that even the Governor of the State had then little idea of the course which he himself was soon about to pursue. If this was the case with the Governor, it could not have been different with thousands of the people. Very soon he became a thorough and uncompromising upholder of the war.

In my proclamation I concurred with the Governor in his determination to preserve the peace and maintain inviolate the honor and integrity of Maryland, and added that I could not withhold my expression of satisfaction at his resolution that no troops should be sent from Maryland to the soil of any other State.

Simultaneously with the passage of the first Northern regiments on their way to Washington, came the news that Virginia had seceded. Two days were crowded with stirring news — a proclamation from the President of the Southern Confederacy offering to issue commissions or letters of marque to privateers, President Lincoln's proclamation declaring a blockade of Southern ports, the Norfolk Navy Yard abandoned, Harper's Ferry evacuated and the arsenal in the hands of Virginia troops. These events, so exciting in themselves, and coming together with the passage of the first troops, greatly increased the danger of an explosion.

CHAPTER IV.

The Sixth Massachusetts Regiment had the honor of being
the first to march in obedience to the call of the President,
completely equipped and organized. It had a full band and
regimental staff. Mustered at Lowell on the morning of the
16th, the day after the proclamation was issued, four companies
from Lowell presented themselves, and to these were added
two from Lawrence, one from Groton, one from Acton, and
one from Worcester; and when the regiment reached Boston,
at one o'clock, an additional company was added from that
city and another from Stoneham, making eleven in all—about
seven hundred men.[1] It was addressed by the Governor of
the State in front of the State House. In the city and along
the line of the railroad, on the 17th, everywhere, ovations
attended them. In the march down Broadway, in New York,
on the 18th, the wildest enthusiasm inspired all classes.
Similar scenes occurred in the progress through New Jersey
and through the city of Philadelphia. At midnight on the
18th, reports reached Philadelphia that the passage of the
regiment through Baltimore would be disputed.

An unarmed and un-uniformed Pennsylvania regiment,
under Colonel Small, was added to the train, either in Phila-

---

[1] Hanson's Sixth Massachusetts Regiment, p. 14.

delphia or when the train reached the Susquehanna — it has been stated both ways, and I am not sure which account is correct — and the two regiments made the force about seventeen hundred men.

The proper course for the Philadelphia, Wilmington and Baltimore Railroad Company was to have given immediate notice to the mayor or board of police of the number of the troops, and the time when they were expected to arrive in the city, so that preparation might have been made to receive them, but no such notice was given. On the contrary, it was purposely withheld, and no information could be obtained from the office of the company, although the marshal of police repeatedly telegraphed to Philadelphia to learn when the troops were to be expected. No news was received until from a half hour to an hour of the time at which they were to arrive. Whatever was the reason that no notice of the approach of the troops was given, it was not because they had no apprehensions of trouble. Mr. Felton, the president of the railroad company, says that *before* the troops left Philadelphia he called the colonel and principal officers into his office, and told them of the dangers they would probably encounter, and advised that each soldier should load his musket before leaving and be ready for any emergency. Colonel Jones's official report, which is dated, "Capitol, Washington, April 22, 1861," says, "*After* leaving Philadelphia, I received intimation that the passage through the city of Baltimore would be resisted. I caused ammunition to be distributed and arms loaded, and went personally through the cars, and issued the following order—viz.:

"'The regiment will march through Baltimore in columns of sections, arms at will. You will undoubtedly be insulted, abused, and perhaps assaulted, to which you must pay no attention whatever, but march with your faces square to the front, and pay no attention to the mob, even if they throw stones, bricks, or other missiles; but if you are fired upon, and any of you are hit, your officers will order you to fire. Do not fire into any promiscuous crowds, but select any man whom you may see aiming at you, and be sure you drop him.'"

If due notice had been given, and if this order had been carried out, the danger of a serious disturbance would have been greatly diminished. The plainest dictates of prudence required the Massachusetts and Pennsylvania regiments to march through the city in a body. The Massachusetts regiment was armed with muskets, and could have defended itself, and would also have had aid from the police; and although the Pennsylvania troops were unarmed, they would have been protected by the police just as troops from the same State had been protected on the day before. The mayor and police commissioners would have been present, adding the sanction and authority of their official positions. But the plan adopted laid the troops open to be attacked in detail when they were least able to defend themselves and were out of the reach of assistance from the police. This plan was that when the train reached the President-street or Philadelphia station, in the southeastern part of Baltimore, each car should, according to custom, be detached from the engine and be drawn through the city by four horses for the distance of more than a mile to the Camden-street or Washington station, in the southwestern part of the city. Some one had blundered.

The train of thirty-five cars arrived at President-street Station at about eleven o'clock. The course which the troops had to take was first northerly on President street, four squares to Pratt street, a crowded thoroughfare leading along the heads of the docks, then along Pratt street west for nearly a mile to Howard street, and then south, on Howard street, one square to the Camden-street station.

Drawn by horses across the city at a rapid pace, about nine[1] cars, containing seven companies of the Massachusetts Sixth, reached the Camden-street station, the first carloads being assailed only with jeers and hisses; but the last car, containing Company "K" and Major Watson, was delayed on its passage—according to one account was thrown off the track by obstructions, and had to be replaced with the help of a passing team; paving-stones and other missiles were thrown, the windows were broken, and some of the soldiers were struck. Colonel Jones was in one of the cars which passed through. Near Gay street, it happened that a number of laborers were at work repaving Pratt street, and had taken up the cobble-stones for the purpose of relaying them. As the troops kept passing, the crowd of bystanders grew larger, the excitement and—among many—the feeling of indignation grew more intense; each new aggressive act was the signal and example for further aggression. A cart coming by with a load of sand, the track was blocked by dumping the cart-load upon it—I have been told that this was the act of some merchants and clerks of the neighborhood—and then, as a more effectual means of obstruction, some anchors lying near the head of the Gay-street dock were dragged up to and placed across the track.[2]

---

[1]According to some of the published accounts *seven* cars got through, which would have been one to each company, but I believe that the number of the cars and of the companies did not correspond. Probably the larger companies were divided.

[2]For participation in placing this obstruction, a wealthy merchant of long experience, usually a very peaceful man, was afterward indicted for treason by the Grand Jury of the Circuit Court of the United States in Baltimore, but his trial was not pressed.

The next car being stopped by these obstructions, the driver attached the horses to the rear end of the car and drove it back, with the soldiers, to the President-street station, the rest of the cars also, of course, having to turn back, or—if any of them had not yet started—to remain where they were at the depot. In the cars thus stopped and turned back there were four companies, " C," " D," " I " and " L," under Captains Follansbee, Hart, Pickering and Dike; also the band, which, I believe, did not leave the depot, and which remained there with the unarmed Pennsylvania regiment. These four companies, in all about 220 men, formed on President street, in the midst of a dense and angry crowd, which threatened and pressed upon the troops, uttering cheers for Jefferson Davis and the Southern Confederacy, and groans for Lincoln and the North, with much abusive language. As the soldiers advanced along President street, the commotion increased; one of the band of rioters appeared bearing a Confederate flag, and it was carried a considerable distance before it was torn from its staff by citizens. Stones were thrown in great numbers, and at the corner of Fawn street two of the soldiers were knocked down by stones and seriously injured. In crossing Pratt-street bridge, the troops had to pick their way over joists and scantling, which by this time had been placed on the bridge to obstruct their passage.

Colonel Jones's official report, from which I have already quoted, thus describes what happened after the four companies left the cars. As Colonel Jones was not present during the march, but obtained the particulars from others, it is not surprising that his account contains errors. These will be pointed out and corrected later:

" They proceeded to march in accordance with orders, and had proceeded but a short distance before they were furiously attacked by a shower of missiles, which came faster as they advanced. They increased their step to double-quick, which seemed to infuriate the mob, as it evidently impressed the mob with the idea that the soldiers dared not fire or had no ammunition, and pistol-shots were numerously fired into the ranks, and one soldier fell dead. The order "Fire!" was given, and it was executed; in consequence several of the mob fell, and the soldiers again advanced hastily. The mayor of Baltimore placed himself at the head of the column beside Captain Follansbee, and proceeded with them a short distance, assuring him that he would protect them, and begging him not to let the men fire. But the mayor's patience was soon exhausted, and he seized a musket from the hands of one of the men, and killed a man therewith; and a policeman, who was in advance of the column, also shot a man with a revolver. They at last reached the cars, and they started immediately for Washington. On going through the train I found there were about one hundred and thirty missing, including the band and field music. Our baggage was seized, and we have not as yet been able to recover any of it. I have found it very difficult to get reliable information in regard to the killed and wounded, but believe there were only three killed.

"As the men went into the cars" [meaning the men who had marched through the city to Camden Station], "I caused the blinds to the cars to be closed, and took every precaution to prevent any shadow of offense to the people of Baltimore, but still the stones flew thick and fast into the train, and it was with the utmost difficulty that I could prevent the troops from leaving the cars and revenging the death of their comrades. After a volley of stones, some one of the soldiers fired and killed a Mr. Davis, who, I ascertained by reliable witnesses, threw a stone into the car." This is incorrectly stated, as will hereafter appear.

It is proper that I should now go back and take up the narration from my own point of view.

On the morning of the 19th of April I was at my law office in Saint Paul street after ten o'clock, when three members of the city council came to me with a message from Marshal Kane, informing me that he had just received intelligence that troops were about to arrive—I did not learn how many —and that he apprehended a disturbance, and requesting me to go to the Camden-street station. I immediately hastened to the office of the board of police, and found that they had received a similar notice. The Counsellor of the City, Mr. George M. Gill, and myself then drove rapidly in a carriage to the Camden-street station. The police commissioners followed, and, on reaching the station, we found Marshal Kane on the ground and the police coming in in squads. A large and angry crowd had assembled, but were restrained by the police from committing any serious breach of the peace.

After considerable delay seven of the eleven companies of the Massachusetts regiment arrived at the station, as already mentioned, and I saw that the windows of the last car were badly broken. No one to whom I applied could inform me whether more troops were expected or not. At this time an alarm was given that the mob was about to tear up the rails in advance of the train on the Washington road, and Marshal Kane ordered some of his men to go out the road as far as necessary to protect the track. Soon afterward, and when I was about to leave the Camden-street station, supposing all danger to be over, news was brought to Police Commissioner Davis and myself, who were standing together, that some troops had been left behind, and that the mob was tearing

up the track on Pratt street, so as to obstruct the progress of
the cars, which were coming to the Camden-street station.
Mr. Davis immediately ran to summon the marshal, who was
at the station with a body of police, to be sent to the point of
danger, while I hastened alone in the same direction. On
arriving at about Smith's Wharf, foot of Gay street, I found
that anchors had been placed on the track, and that Sergeant
McComas and four policemen who were with him were not
allowed by a group of rioters to remove the obstruction. I
at once ordered the anchors to be removed, and my authority
was not resisted. I hurried on, and, approaching Pratt-
street bridge, I saw a battalion, which proved to be four
companies of the Massachusetts regiment which had crossed
the bridge, coming towards me in double-quick time.

They were firing wildly, sometimes backward, over their
shoulders. So rapid was the march that they could not stop
to take aim. The mob, which was not very large, as it seemed
to me, was pursuing with shouts and stones, and, I think, an
occasional pistol-shot. The uproar was furious. I ran at
once to the head of the column, some persons in the crowd
shouting, "Here comes the mayor." I shook hands with the
officer in command, Captain Follansbee, saying as I did so,
"I am the mayor of Baltimore." The captain greeted me
cordially. I at once objected to the double-quick, which was
immediately stopped. I placed myself by his side, and
marched with him. He said, "We have been attacked without provocation," or words to that effect. I replied, "You
must defend yourselves." I expected that he would face his
men to the rear, and, after giving warning, would fire if
necessary. But I said no more, for I immediately felt that,
as mayor of the city, it was not my province to volunteer
such advice. Once before in my life I had taken part in

opposing a formidable riot, and had learned by experience that the safest and most humane manner of quelling a mob is to meet it at the beginning with armed resistance.

The column continued its march. There was neither concert of action nor organization among the rioters. They were armed only with such stones or missiles as they could pick up, and a few pistols. My presence for a short time had some effect, but very soon the attack was renewed with greater violence. The mob grew bolder. Stones flew thick and fast. Rioters rushed at the soldiers and attempted to snatch their muskets, and at least on two occasions succeeded. With one of these muskets a soldier was killed. Men fell on both sides. A young lawyer, then and now known as a quiet citizen, seized a flag of one of the companies and nearly tore it from its staff. He was shot through the thigh, and was carried home apparently a dying man, but he survived to enter the army of the Confederacy, where he rose to the rank of captain, and he afterward returned to Baltimore, where he still lives. The soldiers fired at will. There was no firing by platoons, and I heard no order given to fire. I remember that at the corner of South street several citizens standing in a group fell, either killed or wounded. It was impossible for the troops to discriminate between the rioters and the by-standers, but the latter seemed to suffer most, because, as the main attack was from the mob pursuing the soldiers from the rear, they, in their march, could not easily face backward to fire, but could shoot at those whom they passed on the street. Near the corner of Light street a soldier was severely wounded, who afterward died, and a boy on a vessel lying in the dock was killed, and about the same place three soldiers at the head of the column leveled their muskets and fired into a group standing on the sidewalk, who, as far as I could see, were taking no active part. The shots took effect, bnt I cannot say how many fell. I cried out, waving my umbrella to emphasize my words, " For God's sake don't shoot!" but it was too late. The statement that I begged Captain Follansbee not to let the men fire is incorrect, although on this occasion I did say, " Don't shoot." It then seemed to me that I was in the wrong place, for my presence did not avail to protect either the soldiers or the citizens, and I stepped out from the column. Just at this moment a boy ran forward and handed to me a discharged musket which had fallen from one of the soldiers. I took it from him and hastened into the nearest shop, asking the person in charge to keep it safely, and returned immediately to the street. This boy was far from being alone in his sympathy for the troops, but their friends were powerless, except to care for the wounded and remove the dead. The statement in Colonel Jones's report that I seized a musket and killed one of the rioters is entirely incorrect. The smoking musket seen in my hands was no doubt the foundation for it. There is no foundation for the other statement that one of the police shot a man with a revolver. At the moment when I returned to the street, Marshal Kane, with about fifty policemen (as I then supposed, but I have since ascertained that in fact there were not so many), came at a run from the direction of the Camden-street station, and throwing themselves in the rear of the troops, they formed a line in front of the mob, and with drawn revolvers kept it back. This was between Light and Charles streets. Marshal Kane's voice shouted, " Keep back, men, or I shoot!" This movement, which I saw myself, was gallantly executed, and was perfectly successful. The mob recoiled like water from a rock. One of the leading rioters, then a young man, now a peaceful merchant, tried, as he has himself told me, to pass the line, but the marshal seized him and vowed he would shoot if the attempt was made. This nearly ended the fight, and the column passed on under the protection of the police, without serious molestation, to Camden Station.[1]   I had accompanied the troops for more than a third of a mile, and regarded the danger as now over.   At Camden-street Station there was rioting and confusion.   Commissioner Davis assisted in placing the soldiers in the cars for Washington.   Some muskets were pointed out of the windows by the soldiers.   To this he earnestly objected, as likely to bring on a renewal of the fight, and he advised the blinds to be closed.   The muskets were then withdrawn and the blinds closed, by military order, as stated by Colonel Jones.

At last, about a quarter before one o'clock, the train, consisting of thirteen cars filled with troops, moved out of Camden Station amid the hisses and groans of the multitude, and passed safely on to Washington.   At the outskirts of the city, half a mile or more beyond the station, occurred the unfortunate incident of the killing of Robert W. Davis. This gentleman, a well-known dry-goods merchant, was standing on a vacant lot near the track with two friends, and as the train went by they raised a cheer for Jefferson Davis and the South, when he was immediately shot dead by one of the soldiers from a car-window, several firing at once. There were no rioters near them, and they did not know that the troops had been attacked on their march through the city. There was no "volley of stones" thrown just before Mr. Davis was killed, nor did he or his friends throw any.[2]   This

---

[1] The accounts in some of our newspapers describe serious fighting at a point beyond this, but I am satisfied they are incorrect.

[2] Testimony of witnesses at the coroner's inquest.

was the last of the casualties of the day, and was by far the most serious and unfortunate in its consequences, for it was not unnaturally made the most of to inflame the minds of the people against the Northern troops. Had it not been for this incident, there would perhaps have been among many of our people a keener sense of blame attaching to themselves as the aggressors. Four of the Massachusetts regiment were killed and thirty-six wounded. Twelve citizens were killed, including Mr. Davis. The number of wounded among the latter has never been ascertained. As the fighting was at close quarters, the small number of casualties shows that it was not so severe as has generally been supposed.

But peace even for the day had not come. The unarmed Pennsylvanians and the band of the Massachusetts regiment were still at the President-street station, where a mob had assembled, and the police at that point were not sufficient to protect them. Stones were thrown, and some few of the Pennsylvania troops were hurt, not seriously, I believe. A good many of them were, not unnaturally, seized with a panic, and scattered through the city in different directions. Marshal Kane again appeared on the scene with an adequate force, and an arrangement was made with the railroad company by which the troops were sent back in the direction of Philadelphia. During the afternoon and night a number of stragglers sought the aid of the police and were cared for at one of the station-houses.

The following card of Captain Dike, who commanded Company " C " of the Sixth Massachusetts Regiment, appeared in the Boston *Courier:*

" BALTIMORE, *April* 25, 1861.

" It is but an act of justice that induces me to say to my friends who may feel any interest, and to the community generally, that in the affair which occurred in this city on Friday, the 19th instant, the mayor and city authorities should be exonerated from blame or censure, as they did all in their power, as far as my knowledge extends, to quell the riot, and Mayor Brown attested the sincerity of his desire to preserve the peace, and pass our regiment safely through the city, by marching at the head of its column, and remaining there at the risk of his life. Candor could not permit me to say less, and a desire to place the conduct of the authorities here on the occasion in a right position, as well as to allay feelings, urges me to this sheer act of justice.   JOHN H. DIKE,

" Captain Company ' C,' Seventh Regiment,
attached to Sixth Regiment Massachusetts V. M."

In a letter to Marshal Kane, Colonel Jones wrote as follows :

" HEADQUARTERS SIXTH REGIMENT M. V. M.

" WASHINGTON, D. C., *April* 28, 1861.
" *Marshal Kane, Baltimore, Maryland.*

" Please deliver the bodies of the deceased soldiers belonging to my regiment to Murrill S. Wright, Esq., who is authorized to receive them, and take charge of them through to Boston, and thereby add one more to the many favors for which, in connection with this matter, I am, with my command, much indebted to you. Many, many thanks for the Christian conduct of the authorities of Baltimore in this truly unfortunate affair.

" I am, with much respect, your obedient servant,

"EDWARD F. JONES,
" *Colonel Sixth Regiment M. V. M."*

The following correspondence with the Governor of Massachusetts seems to be entitled to a place in this paper. Gov. Andrew's first telegram cannot be found. The second, which was sent by me in reply, is as follows :

" BALTIMORE, *April* 20, 1861.
" *To the Honorable John A. Andrew, Governor of Massachusetts.*

" *Sir :*—No one deplores the sad events of yesterday in this city more deeply than myself, but they were inevitable. Our people viewed the passage of armed troops to another State through the streets as an invasion of our soil, and could not be restrained. The authorities exerted themselves to the best of their ability, but with only partial success. Governor Hicks was present, and concurs in all my views as to the proceedings now necessary for our protection. When are these scenes to cease? Are we to have a war of sections? God forbid! The bodies of the Massachusetts soldiers could not be sent out to Boston, as you requested, all communication between this city and Philadelphia by railroad and with Boston by steamer having ceased, but they have been placed in cemented coffins, and will be placed with proper funeral ceremonies in the mausoleum of Greenmount Cemetery, where they shall be retained until further directions are received from you. The wounded are tenderly cared for. I appreciate your offer, but Baltimore will claim it as her right to pay all expenses incurred."

" Very respectfully, your obedient servant,
" GEO. WM. BROWN,
" *Mayor of Baltimore.*"

To this the following reply was returned by the Governor :

" *To His Honor George W. Brown, Mayor of Baltimore.*
" *Dear Sir :*—I appreciate your kind attention to our wounded and our dead, and trust that at the earliest moment the remains of our fallen will return to us. I am overwhelmed with surprise that a peaceful march of American citizens over the highway to the defense of our common capital should be deemed aggressive to Baltimoreans. Through New York the march was triumphal. JOHN A. ANDREW,
" *Governor of Massachusetts.*"

This correspondence carries the narrative beyond the nineteenth of April, and I now return to the remaining events of that day.

After the news spread through the city of the fight in the streets, and especially of the killing of Mr. Davis, the excitement became intense. It was manifest that no more troops, while the excitement lasted, could pass through without a bloody conflict. All citizens, no matter what were their political opinions, appeared to agree in this—the strongest friends of the Union as well as its foes. However such a conflict might terminate, the result would be disastrous. In each case it might bring down the vengeance of the North upon the city. If the mob succeeded, it would probably precipitate the city, and perhaps the State, into a temporary secession. Such an event all who had not lost their reason deprecated. The immediate and pressing necessity was that no more troops should arrive.

Governor Hicks called out the military for the preservation of the peace and the protection of the city.

An immense public meeting assembled in Monument Square. Governor Hicks, the mayor, Mr. S. Teackle Wallis, and others, addressed it.

In my speech I insisted on the maintenance of peace and order in the city. I denied that the right of a State to secede from the Union was granted by the Constitution. This was received with groans and shouts of disapproval by a part of the crowd, but I maintained my ground. I deprecated war on the seceding States, and strongly expressed the opinion that the South could not be conquered. I approved of Governor Hicks's determination to send no troops from Maryland to invade the South. I further endeavored to calm the people by informing them of the efforts made by Governor Hicks and myself to prevent the passage of more troops through the city.

Governor Hicks said : " I coincide in the sentiment of your worthy mayor. After three conferences we have agreed, and I bow in submission to the people. I am a Marylander ; I love my State and I love the Union, but I will suffer my right arm to be torn from my body before I will raise it to strike a sister State."

A dispatch had previously been sent by Governor Hicks

and myself to the President of the United States as follows :
" A collision between the citizens and the Northern troops
has taken place in Baltimore, and the excitement is fearful.
Send no troops here. We will endeavor to prevent all
bloodshed. A public meeting of citizens has been called,
and the troops of the State have been called out to preserve
the peace. They will be enough."

Immediately afterward, Messrs. H. Lennox Bond, a
Republican, then Judge of the Criminal Court of Baltimore,
and now Judge of the Circuit Court of the United States;
George W. Dobbin, an eminent lawyer, and John C. Brune,
President of the Board of Trade, went to Washington at my
request, bearing the following letter to the President:

"MAYOR'S OFFICE, BALTIMORE, *April* 19, 1861.

" *Sir :*—This will be presented to you by the Hon. H. Lennox Bond, and
George W. Dobbin, and John C. Brune, Esqs., who will proceed to Washington by an express train at my request, in order to explain fully the
fearful condition of affairs in this city. The people are exasperated to the
highest degree by the passage of troops, and the citizens are universally
decided in the opinion that no more should be ordered to come. The
authorities of the city did their best to-day to protect both strangers and
citizens and to prevent a collision, but in vain, and, but for their great
efforts, a fearful slaughter would have occurred. Under these circumstances it is my solemn duty to inform you that it is not possible for more
soldiers to pass through Baltimore unless they fight their way at every
step. I therefore hope and trust and most earnestly request that no more
troops be permitted or ordered by the Government to pass through the
city. If they should attempt it, the responsibility for the blood shed will
not rest upon me.

" With great respect, your obedient servant,

" GEO. WM. BROWN, *Mayor.*

" *To His Excellency Abraham Lincoln, President United States.*"

To this Governor Hicks added: "I have been in Baltimore
City since Tuesday evening last, and coöperated with Mayor

G. W. Brown in his untiring efforts to allay and prevent the excitement and suppress the fearful outbreak as indicated above, and I fully concur in all that is said by him in the above communication."

No reply came from Washington. The city authorities were left to act on their own responsibility. Late at night reports came of troops being on their way both from Harrisburg and Philadelphia. It was impossible that they could pass through the city without fighting and bloodshed. In this emergency, the board of police, including the mayor, immediately assembled for consultation, and came to the conclusion that it was necessary to burn or disable the bridges on both railroads so far as was required to prevent the ingress of troops. This was accordingly done at once, some of the police and a detachment of the Maryland Guard being sent out to do the work. Governor Hicks was first consulted and urged to give his consent, for we desired that he should share with us the responsibility of taking this grave step. This consent he distinctly gave in my presence and in the presence of several others, and although there was an attempt afterward to deny the fact that he so consented, there can be no doubt whatever about the matter. He was in my house at the time, where, on my invitation, he had taken refuge, thinking that he was in some personal danger at the hotel where he was staying. Early the next morning the Governor returned to Annapolis, and after this the city authorities had to bear alone the responsibilities which the anomalous state of things in Baltimore had brought upon them.

On the Philadelphia Railroad the detachment sent out by special train for the purpose of burning the bridges went as far as the Bush River, and the long bridge there, and the still longer one over the wide estuary of the Gunpowder, a few miles nearer Baltimore, were partially burned. It is an interesting fact that just as this party arrived at the Bush River bridge, a volunteer party of five gentlemen from Baltimore reached the same place on the same errand. They had ridden on horseback by night to the river, and had then gone by boat to the bridge for the purpose of burning it, and in fact they stayed at the bridge and continued the work of burning until the afternoon.

CHAPTER V.

On Saturday morning, the 20th, the excitement and alarm had greatly increased. Up to this time no answer had been received from Washington. The silence became unbearable. Were more troops to be forced through the city at any cost? If so, how were they to come, by land or water? Were the guns of Fort McHenry to be turned upon the inhabitants? Was Baltimore to be compelled at once to determine whether she would side with the North or with the South? Or was she temporarily to isolate herself and wait until the frenzy had in some measure spent its force and reason had begun to resume its sway? In any case it was plain that the author- ities must have the power placed in their hands of controlling any outbreak which might occur. This was the general opinion. Union men and disunion men appeared on the streets with arms in their hands. A time like that predicted in Scripture seemed to have come, when he who had no sword would sell his garment to buy one.

About ten A. M. the city council assembled and immedi- ately appropriated $500,000, to be expended under my direction as mayor, for the purpose of putting the city in a complete state of defense against any description of danger arising or which might arise out of the present crisis. The banks of the city promptly held a meeting, and a few hours afterward a committee appointed by them, consisting of three bank presidents, Johns Hopkins, John Clark and Columbus O'Donnell, all wealthy Union men, placed the whole sum in advance at my disposal. Mr. Scharf, in his "History of Maryland," Volume 3, page 416, says, in a footnote, that this action of the city authorities was endorsed by the editors of the *Sun, American, Exchange, German Correspondent, Clipper, South,* etc. Other considerable sums were contributed by individuals and firms without respect to party.

On the same morning I received a dispatch from Messrs. Bond, Dobbin and Brune, the committee who had gone to Washington, which said: "We have seen the President and General Scott. We have from the former a letter to the mayor and Governor declaring that no troops shall be brought to Baltimore, if, in a military point of view and without interruption from opposition, they can be marched around Baltimore."

As the Governor had left Baltimore for Annapolis early in the morning, I telegraphed him as follows:

"BALTIMORE, *April* 20, 1861.
"*To Governor Hicks.*

"Letter from President and General Scott. No troops to pass through Baltimore if as a military force they can march around. I will answer that every effort will be made to prevent parties leaving the city to molest them, but cannot guarantee against acts of individuals not organized. Do you approve? GEO. WM. BROWN."

This telegram was based on that from Messrs. Bond, Dobbin and Brune. The letter referred to had not been received when my telegram to Governor Hicks was dispatched. I was mistaken in supposing that General Scott had signed the letter as well as the President.

President Lincoln's letter was as follows:

"WASHINGTON, *April* 20, 1861.
" *Governor Hicks and Mayor Brown.*

" *Gentlemen :*—Your letter by Messrs. Bond, Dobbin and Brune is received. I tender you both my sincere thanks for your efforts to keep the peace in the trying situation in which you are placed. For the future troops *must* be brought here, but I make no point of bringing them *through* Baltimore.

" Without any military knowledge myself, of course I must leave details to General Scott. He hastily said this morning, in presence of these gentlemen, ' March them *around* Baltimore, and not through it.'

" I sincerely hope the General, on fuller reflection, will consider this practical and proper, and that you will not object to it.

" By this, a collision of the people of Baltimore with the troops will be avoided unless they go out of their way to seek it. I hope you will exert your influence to prevent this.

" Now and ever I shall do all in my power for peace consistently with the maintenance of government.

"   Your obedient servant,   A. LINCOLN."

Governor Hicks replied as follows to my telegram:

"ANNAPOLIS, *April* 20, 1861.
" *To the Mayor of Baltimore.*

" Your dispatch received. I hoped they would send no more troops through Maryland, but as we have no right to demand that, I am glad no more are to be sent through Baltimore. I know you will do all in your power to preserve the peace.   THOS. H. HICKS."

I then telegraphed to the President as follows:

"BALTIMORE, MARYLAND, *April* 20, 1861.
" *To President Lincoln.*

" Every effort will be made to prevent parties leaving the city to molest troops marching to Washington. Baltimore seeks only to protect herself. Governor Hicks has gone to Annapolis, but I have telegraphed to him.

"GEO. WM. BROWN, *Mayor of Baltimore.*"

After the receipt of the dispatch from Messrs. Bond, Dobbin and Brune, another committee was sent to Washington, consisting of Messrs. Anthony Kennedy, Senator of the United States, and J. Morrison Harris, member of the House of Representatives, both Union men, who sent a dispatch to me saying that they " had seen the President, Secretaries of State, Treasury and War, and also General Scott. The result is the transmission of orders that will stop the passage of troops through or around the city."

Preparations for the defense of the city were nevertheless continued. With this object I issued a notice in which I said : "All citizens having arms suitable for the defense of the city, and which they are willing to contribute for the purpose, are requested to deposit them at the office of the marshal of police."

The board of police enrolled temporarily a considerable number of men and placed them under the command of Colonel Isaac R. Trimble. He informs me that the number amounted to more than fifteen thousand, about three-fourths armed with muskets, shotguns and pistols.

This gentleman was afterward a Major-General in the Confederate Army, where he distinguished himself. He lost a leg at Gettysburg.

By this means not only was the inadequate number of the police supplemented, but many who would otherwise have been the disturbers of the peace became its defenders. And, indeed, not a few of the men enrolled, who thought and hoped that their enrollment meant war, were disappointed to find that the prevention of war was the object of the city authorities, and afterwards found their way into the Confederacy.

For some days it looked very much as if Baltimore had taken her stand decisively with the South ; at all events, the outward expressions of Southern feeling were very emphatic, and the Union sentiment temporarily disappeared.

Early on the morning of Saturday, the 20th, a large Confederate flag floated from the headquarters of a States Rights club on Fayette street near Calvert, and on the afternoon of the same day the Minute Men, a Union club, whose headquarters were on Baltimore street, gave a most significant indication of the strength of the wave of feeling which swept over our people by hauling down the National colors and running up in their stead the State flag of Maryland, amid the cheers of the crowd.[1] Everywhere on the streets men and boys were wearing badges which displayed miniature Confederate flags, and were cheering the Southern cause. Military companies began to arrive from the counties. On Saturday, first came a company of seventy men from Frederick, under Captain Bradley T. Johnson, afterward General in the Southern Army, and next two cavalry companies from Baltimore County, and one from Anne Arundel County. These last, the Patapsco Dragoons, some thirty men, a sturdy-looking body of yeomanry, rode straight to the City Hall and drew up, expecting to be received with a speech of welcome from the mayor. I made them a very brief address, and informed them that dispatches received from Washington had postponed the necessity for their services, whereupon they started homeward amid cheers, their bugler striking up "Dixie," which was the first time I heard that tune. A few days after, they came into Baltimore again. On Sunday came in the Howard County Dragoons, and by steamboat that morning two companies from Talbot County, and soon it was reported that from Harford, Cecil, Carroll and Prince George's, companies were on their way. All the city companies of

---

[1] Baltimore *American*, April 22.

uniformed militia were, of course, under arms. Three batteries of light artillery were in the streets, among them the light field-pieces belonging to the military school at Catonsville, but these the reverend rector of the school, a strong Union man, had thoughtfully spiked.

The United States arsenal at Pikesville, at the time unoccupied, was taken possession of by some Baltimore County troops.

From the local columns of the *American* of the 22d, a paper which was strongly on the Union side, I take the following paragraph:

"WAR SPIRIT ON SATURDAY.

"The war spirit raged throughout the city and among all classes during Saturday with an ardor which seemed to gather fresh force each hour. . . All were united in a determination to resist at every hazard the passage of troops through Baltimore. . . Armed men were marching through the streets, and the military were moving about in every direction, and it is evident that Baltimore is to be the battlefield of the Southern revolution."

And from the *American* of Tuesday, 23d:

"At the works of the Messrs. Winans their entire force is engaged in the making of pikes, and in casting balls of every description for cannon, the steam gun,[1] rifles, muskets, etc., which they are turning out very rapidly."

And a very significant paragraph from the *Sun* of the same day:

" Yesterday morning between 300 and 400 of our most respectable colored residents made a tender of their services

---

[1] Winans's steam gun, a recently invented, and, it was supposed, very formidable engine, was much talked about at this time. It was not very long afterwards seized and confiscated by the military authorities.

to the city authorities.   The mayor thanked them for their offer, and informed them that their services will be called for if they can be made in any way available."

Officers from Maryland in the United States Army were sending in their resignations.   Colonel (afterward General) Huger, of South Carolina, who had recently resigned, and was in Baltimore at the time, was made Colonel of the Fifty-third Regiment, composed of the Independent Greys and the six companies of the Maryland Guard.

On Monday morning, the 22d, I issued an order directing that all the drinking-saloons should be closed that day, and the order was enforced.

On Saturday, April 20th, Captain John C. Robinson, now Major-General, then in command at Fort McHenry, which stands at the entrance of the harbor, wrote to Colonel L. Thomas, Adjutant-General of the United States Army, that he would probably be attacked that night, but he believed he could hold the fort.

In the September number, for the year 1885, of *American History* there is an article written by General Robinson, entitled " Baltimore in 1861," in which he speaks of the apprehended attack on the fort, and of the conduct of the Baltimore authorities.

He says that about nine o'clock on the evening of the 20th, Police Commissioner Davis called at the fort, bringing a letter, dated eight o'clock P. M. of the same evening, from Charles Howard, the president of the board, which he quotes at length, and which states that, from rumors that had reached the board, they were apprehensive that the commander of the fort might be annoyed by lawless and disorderly characters approaching the walls of the fort, and they proposed to send a guard of perhaps two hundred men to station themselves on Whetstone Point, of course beyond the outer limits of the fort, with orders to arrest and hand over to the civil authorities any evil-disposed and disorderly persons who might approach the fort. The letter further stated that this duty would have been confided to the police force, but their services were so imperatively required elsewhere that it would be impossible to detail a sufficient number, and this duty had therefore been entrusted to a detachment of the regular organized militia of the State, then called out pursuant to law, and actually in the service of the State. It was added that the commanding officer of the detachment would be ordered to communicate with Captain Robinson. The letter closed with repeating the assurance verbally given to Captain Robinson in the morning that no disturbance at or near the post should be made with the sanction of any of the constituted authorities of the city of Baltimore; but, on the contrary, all their powers should be exerted to prevent anything of the kind by any parties. A postscript stated that there might perhaps be a troop of volunteer cavalry with the detachment.

General Robinson continues :

" I did not question the good faith of Mr. Howard, but Commissioner Davis verbally stated that they proposed to send the Maryland Guards to help protect the fort. Having made the acquaintance of some of the officers of that organization, and heard them freely express their opinions, I declined the offered support, and then the following conversation occurred :

" *Commandant.* I am aware, sir, that we are to be attacked to-night. I received notice of it before sundown. If you will go outside with me you will see we are prepared for it. You will find the guns loaded, and men standing by them. As for the Maryland Guards, they cannot come here. I am acquainted with some of those gentlemen, and know what their sentiments are.

" *Commissioner Davis.* Why, Captain, we are anxious to avoid a collision.

" *Commandant.* So am I, sir. If you wish to avoid a collision, place your city military anywhere between the city and that chapel on the road, but if they come this side of it, I shall fire on them.

"*Commissioner Davis.*   Would you fire into the city of Baltimore?

"*Commandant.*   I should be sorry to do it, sir, but if it becomes necessary in order to hold this fort, I shall not hesitate for one moment.

"*Commissioner Davis* (excitedly).   I assure you, Captain Robinson, if there is a woman or child killed in that city, there will not be one of you left alive here, sir.

"*Commandant.*   Very well, sir, I will take the chances.   Now, I assure you, Mr. Davis, if your Baltimore mob comes down here to-night, you will not have another mob in Baltimore for ten years to come, sir."

Mr. Davis is a well-known and respected citizen of Baltimore, who has filled various important public offices with credit, and at present holds a high position in the Baltimore and Ohio Railroad Company.   According to his recollection, the interview was more courteous and less dramatic than would be supposed from the account given by General Robinson. Mr. Davis says that the people of Baltimore were acquainted with the defenseless condition of the fort, and that in the excited state of the public mind this fact probably led to the apprehension and consequent rumor that an attempt would be made to capture it.   The police authorities believed, and, as it turned out, correctly, that the rumor was without foundation; yet, to avoid the danger of any disturbance whatever, the precautions were taken which are described in the letter of Mr. Howard, and Mr. Davis went in person to deliver it to Captain Robinson.

His interview was not, however, confined to Captain Robinson, but included also other officers of the fort, and Mr. Davis was hospitably received.   A conversation ensued in regard to the threatened attack, and, with one exception, was conducted without asperity.   A junior officer threatened, in case of an attack, to direct the fire of a cannon on the Washington Monument, which stands in the heart of the city, and to this threat Mr. Davis replied with heat, "If you do that, and if a woman or child is killed, there will be nothing left of you but your brass buttons to tell who you were."

The commandant insisted that the military sent by the board should not approach the fort nearer than the Roman Catholic chapel, a demand to which Mr. Davis readily assented, as that situation commanded the only approach from the city to the fort. In the midst of the conversation the long roll was sounded, and the whole garrison rushed to arms. For a long time, and until the alarm was over, Mr. Davis was left alone.

General Robinson was mistaken in his conjecture, "when it seemed to him that for hours of the night mounted men from the country were crossing the bridges of the Patapsco." There was but one bridge over the Patapsco, known as the Long Bridge, from which any sound of passing horsemen or vehicles of any description could possibly have been heard at the fort. The sounds which did reach the fort from the Long Bridge during the hours of the night were probably the market wagons of Anne Arundel County passing to and from the city on their usual errand, and the one or two companies from that county, which came to Baltimore during the period of disturbance, no doubt rode in over the Long Bridge by daylight.

General Robinson, after describing in his paper the riot of the 19th of April and the unfortunate event of the killing of Mr. Davis, adds: "It is impossible to describe the intense excitement that now prevailed. Only those who saw and felt it can understand or conceive any adequate idea of its extent"; and in this connection he mentions the fact that Marshal Kane, chief of the police force, on the evening of the 19th of April, telegraphed to Bradley T. Johnson, at

Frederick, as follows : "Streets red with Maryland blood; send expresses over the mountains of Maryland and Virginia for the riflemen to come without delay.   Fresh hordes will be down on us to-morrow.   We will fight them and whip them, or die."

The sending of this dispatch was indeed a startling event, creating a new complication and embarrassing in the highest degree to the city authorities.   The marshal of police, who had gallantly and successfully protected the national troops on the 18th and 19th, was so carried away by the frenzy of the hour that he had thus on his own responsibility summoned volunteers from Virginia and Maryland to contest the passage of national troops through the city.   Different views were taken by members of the board of police.   It was considered, on the one hand, that the services of Colonel Kane were, in that crisis, indispensable, because no one could control as he could the secession element of the city, which was then in the ascendant and might get control of the city, and, on the other, that his usefulness had ceased, because not only had the gravest offense been given to the Union sentiment of the city by this dispatch, but the authorities in Washington, while he was at the head of the police, could no longer have any confidence in the police, or perhaps in the board itself.   The former consideration prevailed.

It is due to Marshal Kane to say that subsequently, and while he remained in office, he performed his duty to the satisfaction of the Board.   Some years after the war was over he was elected sheriff, and still later mayor of the city, and in both capacities he enjoyed the respect and regard of the community.

It may with propriety be added that the conservative position and action of the police board were so unsatisfactory to many of the more heated Southern partisans, that a scheme was at one time seriously entertained by them to suppress the board, and transfer the control of the police force to other hands. Happily for all parties, better counsels prevailed.

On Sunday, the 21st of April, with three prominent citizens of Baltimore, I went to Washington, and we there had an interview with the President and Cabinet and General Scott. This interview was of so much importance, that a statement of what occurred was prepared on the same day and was immediately published. It is here given at length:

BALTIMORE, *April* 21.

Mayor Brown received a dispatch from the President of the United States at three o'clock A. M. (this morning), directed to himself and Governor Hicks, requesting them to go to Washington by special train, in order to consult with Mr. Lincoln for the preservation of the peace of Maryland. The mayor replied that Governor Hicks was not in the city, and inquired if he should go alone. Receiving an answer by telegraph in the affirmative, his Honor, accompanied by George W. Dobbin, John C. Brune and S. T. Wallis, Esqs., whom he had summoned to attend him, proceeded at once to the station. After a series of delays they were enabled to procure a special train about half-past seven o'clock, in which they arrived at Washington about ten.

They repaired at once to the President's house, where they were admitted to an immediate interview, to which the Cabinet and General Scott were summoned. A long conversation and discussion ensued. The President, upon his part, recognized the good faith of the city and State authorities, and insisted upon his own. He admitted the excited state of feeling in Baltimore, and his desire and duty to avoid the fatal consequences of a collision with the people. He urged, on the other hand, the absolute, irresistible necessity of having a transit through the State for such troops as might be necessary for the protection of the Federal capital. The protection of Washington, he asserted with great earnestness, was the sole object of concentrating troops there, and he protested that none of the troops brought through Maryland were intended for any purposes hostile to the State, or aggressive as against the Southern States. Being now unable to bring them up the Potomac in security, the President must either bring them through Maryland or abandon the capital.

He called on General Scott for his opinion, which the General gave at length, to the effect that troops might be brought through Maryland without going through Baltimore, by either carrying them from Perryville to Annapolis, and thence by rail to Washington, or by bringing them to the Relay House on the Northern Central Railroad [about seven miles north of the city], and marching them to the Relay House on the Washington Railroad [about seven miles south-west of the city], and thence by rail to the capital. If the people would permit them to go by either of these routes uninterruptedly, the necessity of their passing through Baltimore would be avoided. If the people would not permit them a transit thus remote from the city, they must select their own best route, and, if need be, fight their own way through Baltimore—a result which the General earnestly deprecated.

The President expressed his hearty concurrence in the desire to avoid a collision, and said that no more troops should be ordered through Baltimore if they were permitted to go uninterrupted by either of the other routes suggested. In this disposition the Secretary of War expressed his participation.

Mayor Brown assured the President that the city authorities would use all lawful means to prevent their citizens from leaving Baltimore to attack the troops in passing at a distance ; but he urged, at the same time, the impossibility of their being able to promise anything more than their best efforts in that direction. The excitement was great, he told the President, the people of all classes were fully aroused, and it was impossible for any one to answer for the consequences of the presence of Northern troops anywhere within our borders. He reminded the President also that the jurisdiction of the city authorities was confined to their own population, and that he could give no promises for the people elsewhere, because he would be unable to keep them if given. The President frankly acknowledged this difficulty, and said that the Government would only ask the city authorities to use their best efforts with respect to those under their jurisdiction.

The interview terminated with the distinct assurance on the part of the President that no more troops would be sent through Baltimore, unless obstructed in their transit in other directions, and with the understanding that the city authorities should do their best to restrain their own people.

The Mayor and his companions availed themselves of the President's full discussion of the day to urge upon him respectfully, but in the most earnest manner, a course of policy which would give peace to the country, and especially the withdrawal of all orders contemplating the passage of troops through any part of Maryland.

On returning to the cars, and when just about to leave, about 2 P. M., the Mayor received a dispatch from Mr. Garrett (the President of the Baltimore and Ohio Railroad) announcing the approach of troops to Cockeysville [about fourteen miles from Baltimore on the Northern Central Railroad], and the excitement consequent upon it in the city. Mr. Brown and his companions returned at once to the President and asked an immediate audience, which was promptly given. The Mayor exhibited Mr. Garrett's dispatch, which gave the President great surprise. He immediately summoned the Secretary of War and General Scott, who soon appeared with other members of the Cabinet. The dispatch was submitted. The President at once, in the most decided way, urged the recall of the troops, saying he had no idea they would be there. Lest there should be the slightest suspicion of bad faith on his part in summoning the Mayor to Washington and allowing troops to march on the city during his absence, he desired that the troops should, if it were practicable, be sent back at once to York or Harrisburg. General Scott adopted the President's views warmly, and an order was accordingly prepared by the Lieutenant-General to that effect, and forwarded by Major Belger, of the Army, who also accompanied the Mayor to this city. The troops at Cockeysville, the Mayor was assured, were not brought there for transit through the city, but were intended to be marched to the Relay House on the Baltimore and Ohio Railroad. They will proceed to Harrisburg, from there to Philadelphia, and thence by the Chesapeake and Delaware Canal or by Perryville, as Major-General Patterson may direct.

This statement is made by the authority of the Mayor and Messrs. George W. Dobbin, John C. Brune and S. T. Wallis, who accompanied Mr. Brown, and who concurred with him in all particulars in the course adopted by him in the two interviews with Mr. Lincoln.

GEO. WM. BROWN, Mayor.

This statement was written by Mr. Wallis, at the request of his associates, on the train, and was given to the public immediately on their return to the city.

In the course of the first conversation Mr. Simon Cameron called my attention to the fact that an iron bridge on the Northern Central Railway, which, he remarked, belonged to the city of Baltimore, had been disabled by a skilled person so as to inflict little injury on the bridge, and he desired to know by what authority this had been done. Up to this time nothing had been said about the disabling of the bridges. In reply I addressed myself to the President, and said, with much earnestness, that the disabling of this bridge, and of the other bridges, had been done by authority, as the reader has already been told, and that it was a measure of protection on a sudden emergency, designed to prevent bloodshed in the city of Baltimore, and not an act of hostility towards the General Government; that the people of Maryland had always been deeply attached to the Union, which had been shown on all occasions, but that they, including the citizens of Baltimore, regarded the proclamation calling for 75,000 troops as an act of war on the South, and a violation of its constitutional rights, and that it was not surprising that a high-spirited people, holding such opinions, should resent the passage of Northern troops through their city for such a purpose.

Mr. Lincoln was greatly moved, and, springing up from his chair, walked backward and forward through the apartment. He said, with great feeling, " Mr. Brown, I am not a learned man! I am not a learned man!" that his proclamation had not been correctly understood ; that he had no intention of bringing on war, but that his purpose was to defend the capital, which was in danger of being bombarded from the heights across the Potomac.

I am giving here only a part of a frank and full conversation, in which others present participated.

The telegram of Mr. Garrett to me referred to in the preceding statement is in the following words : " Three thousand Northern troops are reported to be at Cockeysville. Intense excitement prevails. Churches have been dismissed and the people are arming in mass. To prevent terrific bloodshed, the result of your interview and arrangement is awaited."

To this the following reply to Mr. Garrett was made by me :
" Your telegram received on our return from an interview
with the President, Cabinet and General Scott. Be calm and
do nothing until you hear from me again. I return to see
the President at once and will telegraph again. Wallis,
Brune and Dobbin are with me."

Accordingly, after the second interview, the following dispatch was sent by me to Mr. Garrett : " We have again seen
the President, General Scott, Secretary of War and other
members of the Cabinet, and the troops are ordered to return
forthwith to Harrisburg. A messenger goes with us from
General Scott. We return immediately."

Mr. Garrett's telegram was not exaggerated. It was a
fearful day in Baltimore. Women and children, and men,
too, were wild with excitement. A certainty of a fight in
the streets if Northern troops should enter was the pressing
danger. Those who were arming in hot haste to resist the
passage of Northern troops little recked of the fearful risk to
which they were exposing themselves and all they held dear.
It was well for the city and State that the President had
decided as he did. When the President gave his deliberate
decision that the troops should pass around Baltimore and
not through it, General Scott, stern soldier as he sometimes
was, said with emotion, " Mr. President, I thank you for
this, and God will bless you for it."

From the depth of our hearts my colleagues and myself
thanked both the General and the President.

The troops on the line of the Northern Central Railway—
some 2400 men, about half of them armed—did not receive
their orders to return to Pennsylvania until after several
days. As they had expected to make the journey to Washington by rail, they were naturally not well equipped or

supplied for camp life. I take the following from the *Sun* of April 23d : " By order of Marshal Kane, several wagon-loads of bread and meat were sent to the camp of the Pennsylvania troops, it being understood that a number were sick and suffering for proper food and nourishment. . . . One of the Pennsylvanians died on Sunday and was buried within the encampment. Two more died yesterday and a number of others were on the sick list. The troops were deficient in food, having nothing but crackers to feed upon."

The Eighth Massachusetts Regiment, under command of General Butler, was the next which passed through Maryland. It reached Perryville, on the Susquehanna, by rail on the 20th, and there embarked on the steamboat *Maryland,* arriving at Annapolis early on the morning of the 21st. Governor Hicks addressed the General a note advising that he should not land his men, on account of the great excitement there, and stated that he had telegraphed to that effect to the Secretary of War.

The Governor also wrote to the President, advising him to order elsewhere the troops then off Annapolis, and to send no more through Maryland, and added the surprising suggestion that Lord Lyons, the British Minister, be requested to act as mediator between the contending parties of the country.

The troops, however, were landed without opposition. The railway from Annapolis leading to the Washington road had, in some places, been torn up, but it was promptly repaired by the soldiers, and by the 25th an unobstructed route was opened through Annapolis to Washington.

Horace Greeley, in his book called " The American Conflict," denounces with characteristic vehemence and severity of language the proceedings of the city authorities. He scouts " the demands" of the Mayor and his associates, whom he designates as " Messrs. Brown & Co." He insists that practically on the morning of the 20th of April Maryland was a member of the Southern Confederacy, and that her Governor spoke and acted the bidding of a cabal of the ablest and most envenomed traitors.

It is true that the city then, and for days afterwards, was in an anomalous condition, which may be best described as one of " armed neutrality "; but it is not true that in any sense it was, on the 20th of April, or at any other time, a member of the Southern Confederacy. On the contrary, while many, especially among the young and reckless, were doing their utmost to place it in that position, regardless of consequences, and would, if they could, have forced the hands of the city authorities, it was their conduct which prevented such a catastrophe. Temporizing and delay were necessary. As soon as passions had time to cool, a strong reaction set in and the people rapidly divided into two parties—one on the side of the North, and the other on the side of the South; but whatever might be their personal or political sympathies, it was clear to all who had not lost their reason that Maryland, which lay open from the North by both land and sea, would be kept in the Union for the sake of the national capital, even if it required the united power of the nation to accomplish the object. The telegraph wires on the lines leading to the North had been cut, and for some days the city was without regular telegraphic connection. For a longer time the mails were interrupted and travel was stopped. The buoys in the harbor were temporarily removed. The business interests of the city of course suffered under these interruptions, and would be paralyzed if such isolation were to continue, and the merchants soon began to demand that the channels of trade should be reopened to the north and east.

The immediate duty of the city authorities was to keep the peace and protect the city, and, without going into details or discussing the conduct of individuals, I shall leave others to speak of the manner in which it was performed.

Colonel Scharf, in his " History of Maryland," Volume III, p. 415, sums up the matter as follows: " In such a period of intense excitement, many foolish and unnecessary acts were undoubtedly done by persons in the employment of the city, as well as by private individuals, but it is undoubtedly true that the Mayor and board of police commissioners were inflexibly determined to resist all attempts to force the city into secession or into acts of hostility to the Federal Government, and that they successfully accomplished their purpose. If they had been otherwise disposed, they could easily have effected their object."

CHAPTER VI.

On the 22d of April, Governor Hicks convened the General Assembly of the State, to meet in special session at
Annapolis on the 26th, to deliberate and consider of the condition of the State, and to take such measures as in their
wisdom they might deem fit to maintain peace and order and
security within its limits.

On the 24th of April, " in consequence of the extraordinary
state of affairs," Governor Hicks changed the meeting of
the Assembly to Frederick. The candidates for the House
of Delegates for the city of Baltimore, who had been returned
as elected to the General Assembly in 1859, had been refused
their seats, as previously stated, and a new election in the
city had therefore become necessary to fill the vacancy.

A special election for that purpose was accordingly held in
the city on the 24th instant. Only a States Rights ticket was
presented, for which nine thousand two hundred and forty-
four votes were cast. The candidates elected were : John C.
Brune, Ross Winans, Henry M. Warfield, J. Hanson
Thomas, T. Parkin Scott, H. M. Morfit, S. Teackle Wallis,

Charles H. Pitts, William G. Harrison and Lawrence Sangston, well-known and respected citizens, and the majority of them nominated because of their known conservatism and declared opposition to violent measures.

This General Assembly, which contained men of unusual weight and force of character, will ever remain memorable in Maryland for the courage and ability with which it maintained the constitutional rights of the State.

On the 3d of May, the board of police made a report of its proceedings to the Legislature of the State, signed by Charles Howard, President. After speaking of the disabling of the railroads, it concludes as follows:

" The absolute necessity of the measures thus determined upon by the Governor, Mayor and Police Board, is fully illustrated by the fact that early on Sunday morning reliable information reached the city of the presence of a large body of Pennsylvania troops, amounting to about twenty-four hundred men, who had reached Ashland, near Cockeysville, by the way of the Northern Central Railroad, and was stopped in their progress towards Baltimore by the partial destruction of the Ashland bridge. Every intelligent citizen at all acquainted with the state of feeling then existing, must be satisfied that if these troops had attempted to march through the city, an immense loss of life would have ensued in the conflict which would necessarily have taken place. The bitter feelings already engendered would have been intensely increased by such a conflict ; all attempts at conciliation would have been vain, and terrible destruction would have been the consequence, if, as is certain, other bodies of troops had insisted on forcing their way through the city.

" The tone of the whole Northern press and the mass of the population was violent in the extreme. Incursions upon our city were daily threatened, not only by troops in the service of the Federal Government, but by the vilest and most reckless desperadoes, acting independently, and, as they threatened, in despite of the Government, backed by well-known influential citizens, and sworn to the commission of all kinds of excesses. In short, every possible effort was made to alarm this community. In this condition of things the Board felt it to be their solemn duty to continue the organization which had already been commenced, for the purpose of assuring the people of

Baltimore that no effort would be spared to protect all within its borders, to the extent of their ability. All the means employed were devoted to this end, and with no view of producing a collision with the General Government, which the Board were particularly anxious to avoid, and an arrangement was happily effected by the Mayor with the General Government that no troops should be passed through the city. As an evidence of the determination of the Board to prevent such collision, a sufficient guard was sent in the neighborhood of Fort McHenry several nights to arrest all parties who might be engaged in a threatened attack upon it, and a steam-tug was employed, properly manned, to prevent any hostile demonstration upon the receiving-ship *Alleghany*, lying at anchor in the harbor, of all which the United States officers in command were duly notified.

" Property of various descriptions belonging to the Government and individuals was taken possession of by the police force with a view to its security. The best care has been taken of it. Every effort has been made to discover the rightful owners, and a portion of it has already been forwarded to order. Arrangements have been made with the Government agents satisfactory to them for the portion belonging to it, and the balance is held subject to the order of its owners.

" Amidst all the excitement and confusion which has since prevailed, the Board take great pleasure in stating that the good order and peace of the city have been preserved to an extraordinary degree. Indeed, to judge from the accounts given by the press of other cities of what has been the state of things in their own communities, Baltimore, during the whole of the past week and up to this date, will compare favorably, as to the protection which persons and property have enjoyed, with any other large city in the United States."

Much has been said in regard to the suppression of the national flag in Baltimore during the disturbances, and it is proper that the facts should here be stated.

General Robinson, in his description of the occurrences which took place after the 19th of April, says that meetings were held under the flag of the State of Maryland, at which the speeches were inflammatory secession harangues, and that the national flag disappeared, and no man dared to display it. Whether or not this statement exactly represents the condition of things, it at least approximates it, and on the 26th of April, an order was issued by the board of police reciting that the peace of the city was likely to be disturbed by the display of various flags, and directing that no flag of any description should be raised or carried through the streets. On April 29th, the city council passed an ordinance, signed by the Mayor, authorizing him, when in his opinion the peace of the city required it, to prohibit by proclamation for a limited period, to be designated by him, the public display of all flags or banners in the city of Baltimore, except on buildings or vessels occupied or employed by the Government of the United States. On the same day I, in pursuance of the ordinance, issued a proclamation prohibiting the display of flags for thirty days, with the exception stated in the ordinance, and on the 10th of May, when I was satisfied that all danger was over, I issued a proclamation removing the prohibition. The only violation of the order which came under my notice during the period of suppression was on the part of a military company which had the Maryland flag flying at its headquarters, on Lexington street near the City Hall. On my directing this flag to be taken down, the request was at once complied with.

General Robinson says that "the first demonstration of returning loyalty was on the 28th day of April, when a sailing vessel came down the river crowded with men, and covered from stem to stern with national flags. She sailed past the fort, cheered and saluted our flag, which was dipped in return, after which she returned to the city." He then adds: "The tide had turned. Union men avowed themselves, the stars and stripes were again unfurled, and order was restored. Although after this time arrests were made of persons conspicuous for disloyalty, the return to reason was almost as sudden as the outbreak of rebellion. The railroads were repaired, trains ran regularly, and troops poured into Washington without hindrance or opposition of any sort. Thousands of men volunteered for the Union Army. Four regiments of Maryland troops afterwards served with me, and constituted the Third Brigade of my division. They fought gallantly the battles of the Union, and no braver soldiers ever marched under the flag."

The tide indeed soon turned, but not quite so rapidly as this statement seems to indicate. On the 5th of May, General Butler, with two regiments and a battery of artillery, came from Washington and took possession of the Relay House on the Baltimore and Ohio Railroad at the junction of the Washington branch, about seven miles from Baltimore, and fortified the position. One of his first proceedings was highly characteristic. He issued a special order declaring that he had found well-authenticated evidence that one of his soldiers had "been poisoned by means of strychnine administered in the food brought into the camp," and he warned the people of Maryland that he could "put an agent, with a word, into every household armed with this terrible weapon." This statement sent a thrill of horror through the North, and the accompanying threat of course excited the indignation and disgust of our people. The case was carefully examined by the city physician, and it turned out that the man had an ordinary attack of cholera morbus, the consequence of imprudent diet and camp life, but the General never thought proper to correct the slander.

On the evening of the 11th of May, General Butler being then at Annapolis, I received a note from Edward G. Parker, his aide-de-camp, stating that he had received intimations from many sources that an attack by the Baltimore roughs

was intended that night; that these rumors had been confirmed by a gentleman from Baltimore, who gave his name
and residence; that the attack would be made by more than
a thousand men, every one sworn to kill a man; that they
were coming in wagons, on horses and on foot, and that a
considerable force from the west, probably the Point of
Rocks in Maryland, was also expected, and I was requested
to guard every avenue from the city, so as to prevent the
Baltimore rioters from leaving town.

Out of respect to the source from which the application
came, I immediately sent for the marshal of police, and
requested him to throw out bodies of his men so as to guard
every avenue leading to the Relay House. No enemy, however, appeared. The threatened attack proved to be merely
a groundless alarm, as I knew from the beginning it was.

On the night of the 13th of May, when the city was as
peaceful as it is to-day, General Butler, in the midst of a
thunderstorm of unusual violence, entered Baltimore and
took possession of Federal Hill, which overlooks the harbor
and commands the city, and which he immediately proceeded
to fortify. There was nobody to oppose him, and nobody
thought of doing so; but, for this exploit, which he regarded
as the capture of Baltimore, he was made a Major-General.
He immediately issued a proclamation, as if he were in a
conquered city subject to military law.

Meantime, on the 26th of April, the General Assembly of
the State had met at Frederick. "As soon as the General
Assembly met" (Scharf's History of Maryland, Vol. III,
p. 444), "the Hon. James M. Mason, formerly United States
Senator from Virginia, waited on it as commissioner from that
State, authorized to negotiate a treaty of alliance offensive
and defensive with Maryland on her behalf." This proposi-

tion met with no acceptance. On the 27th, the Senate, by a unanimous vote, issued an address for the purpose of allaying the apprehensions of the people, declaring that it had no constitutional authority to take any action leading to secession, and on the next day the House of Delegates, by a vote of 53 to 12, made a similar declaration. Early in May, the General Assembly, by a vote in the House of 43 to 12, and in the Senate of 11 to 3, passed a series of resolutions proclaiming its position in the existing crisis.

The resolutions protested against the war as unjust and unconstitutional, and announced a determination to take no part in its prosecution. They expressed a desire for the immediate recognition of the Confederate States; and while they protested against the military occupation of the State, and the arbitrary restrictions and illegalities with which it was attended, they called on all good citizens to abstain from violent and unlawful interference with the troops, and patiently and peacefully to leave to time and reason the ultimate and certain re-establishment and vindication of the right; and they declared it to be at that time inexpedient to call a Sovereign Convention of the State, or to take any measures for the immediate organization or arming of the militia.

After it became plain that no movement would be made towards secession, a large number of young men, including not a few of the flower of the State, and representing largely the more wealthy and prominent families, escaped across the border and entered the ranks of the Confederacy. The number has been estimated at as many as twenty thousand, but this, perhaps, is too large a figure, and there are no means of ascertaining the truth. The muster-rolls have perished with the Confederacy. The great body of those who sympathized with the South had no disposition to take arms against the Union so long as Maryland remained a member of it. This was subsequently proved by their failure to enlist in the Southern armies on the different occasions in 1862, 1863 and 1864 when they crossed the Potomac and transferred the seat of war to Maryland and Pennsylvania, under the command twice of General Lee and once of General Early.

The first of these campaigns ended in the bloody battle of Antietam. The Maryland men, as a tribute to their good conduct, were placed at the head of the army, and crossed the river with enthusiasm, the band playing and the soldiers singing " My Maryland." Great was their disappointment that the recruits did not even suffice to fill the gaps in their shattered ranks.

CHAPTER VII.

The suspension of the writ of *habeas corpus*, by order of
the President, without the sanction of an Act of Congress,
which had not then been given, was one of the memorable
events of the war.

On the 4th of May, 1861, Judge Giles, of the United States
District Court of Maryland, issued a writ of *habeas corpus* to
Major Morris, then in command of Fort McHenry, to discharge a soldier who was under age. Major Morris refused
to obey the writ.

On the 14th of May the General Assembly adjourned, and
Mr. Ross Winans, of Baltimore, a member of the House of
Delegates, while returning to his home, was arrested by
General Butler on a charge of high treason. He was con-
veyed to Annapolis, and subsequently to Fort McHenry, and
was soon afterwards released.

A case of the highest importance next followed. On the
25th of May, Mr. John Merryman, of Baltimore County, was
arrested by order of General Keim, of Pennsylvania, and confined in Fort McHenry. The next day (Sunday, May 26th)
his counsel, Messrs. George M. Gill and George H. Williams,
presented a petition for the writ of *habeas corpus* to Chief
Justice Taney, who issued the writ immediately, directed

to General Cadwallader, then in command in Maryland, ordering him to produce the body of Merryman in court on the following day (Monday, May 27th).   On that day Colonel Lee, his aide-de-camp, came into court with a letter from General Cadwallader, directed to the Chief Justice, stating that Mr. Merryman had been arrested on charges of high treason, and that he (the General) was authorized by the President of the United States in such cases to suspend the writ of *habeas corpus* for the public safety.   Judge Taney asked Colonel Lee if he had brought with him the body of John Merryman.   Colonel Lee replied that he had no instructions except to deliver the letter.

> *Chief Justice.*—The commanding officer, then, declines to obey the writ?
> *Colonel Lee.*—After making that communication my duty is ended, and I have no further power (rising and retiring).
> *Chief Justice.*—The Court orders an attachment to issue against George Cadwallader for disobedience to the high writ of the Court, returnable at twelve o'clock to-morrow.

The order was accordingly issued as directed.

A startling issue was thus presented.   The venerable Chief Justice had come from Washington to Baltimore for the purpose of issuing a writ of *habeas corpus*, and the President had thereupon authorized the commander of the fort to hold the prisoner and disregard the writ.

A more important occasion could hardly have occurred. Where did the President of the United States acquire such a power?   Was it true that a citizen held his liberty subject to the arbitrary will of any man?   In what part of the Constitution could such a power be found?   Why had it never been discovered before?   What precedent existed for such an act?

Judge Taney was greatly venerated in Baltimore, where

he had formerly lived. The case created a profound sensation.

On the next morning the Chief Justice, leaning on the arm of his grandson, walked slowly through the crowd which had gathered in front of the court-house, and the crowd silently and with lifted hats opened the way for him to pass.

Roger B. Taney was one of the most self-controlled and courageous of judges. He took his seat with his usual quiet dignity. He called the case of John Merryman and asked the marshal for his return to the writ of attachment. The return stated that he had gone to Fort McHenry for the purpose of serving the writ on General Cadwallader; that he had sent in his name at the outer gate; that the messenger had returned with the reply that there was no answer to send; that he was not permitted to enter the gate, and, therefore, could not serve the writ, as he was commanded to do.

The Chief Justice then read from his manuscript as follows:

I ordered the attachment of yesterday because upon the face of the return the detention of the prisoner was unlawful upon two grounds:

1st. The President, under the Constitution and laws of the United States, cannot suspend the privilege of the writ of *habeas corpus*, nor authorize any military officer to do so.

2d. A military officer has no right to arrest and detain a person not subject to the rules and articles of war, for an offense against the laws of the United States, except in aid of the judicial authority and subject to its control; and if the party is arrested by the military, it is the duty of the officer to deliver him over immediately to the civil authority, to be dealt with according to law.

I forbore yesterday to state the provisions of the Constitution of the United States which make these principles the fundamental law of the Union, because an oral statement might be misunderstood in some portions of it, and I shall therefore put my opinion in writing, and file it in the office of the clerk of this court, in the course of this week.

The Chief Justice then orally remarked:

In relation to the present return, it is proper to say that of course the marshal has legally the power to summon the *posse comitatus* to seize and bring into court the party named in the attachment; but it is apparent he will be resisted in the discharge of that duty by a force notoriously superior to the *posse*, and, this being the case, such a proceeding can result in no good, and is useless. I will not, therefore, require the marshal to perform this duty. If, however, General Cadwallader were before me, I should impose on him the punishment which it is my province to inflict—that of fine and imprisonment. I shall merely say, to-day, that I shall reduce to writing the reasons under which I have acted, and which have led me to the conclusions expressed in my opinion, and shall direct the clerk to forward them with these proceedings to the President, so that he may discharge his constitutional duty "to take care that the laws are faithfully executed."

It is due to my readers that they should have an opportunity of reading this opinion, and it is accordingly inserted in an Appendix.

After the court had adjourned, I went up to the bench and thanked Judge Taney for thus upholding, in its integrity, the writ of *habeas corpus*. He replied, "Mr. Brown, I am an old man, a very old man" (he had completed his eighty-fourth year), "but perhaps I was preserved for this occasion." I replied, "Sir, I thank God that you were."

He then told me that he knew that his own imprisonment had been a matter of consultation, but that the danger had passed, and he warned me, from information he had received, that my time would come.

The charges against Merryman were discovered to be unfounded and he was soon discharged by military authority.

The nation is now tired of war, and rests in the enjoyment of a harmony which has not been equalled since the days of James Monroe. When Judge Taney rendered this decision the Constitution was only seventy-two years old—twelve years younger than himself. It is now less than one hundred years old—a short period in a nation's life—and yet during that period there have been serious commotions—two foreign wars and a civil war. In the future, as in the past, offenses will come, and hostile parties and factions will arise, and the men who wield power will, if they dare, shut up in fort or prison, without reach of relief, those whom they regard as dangerous enemies. When that period arrives, then will those who wisely love their country thank the great Chief Justice, as I did, for his unflinching defense of *habeas corpus*, the supreme writ of right, and the corner-stone of personal liberty among all English-speaking people.

In the Life of Benjamin R. Curtis, Vol. I, p. 240, his biographer says, speaking of Chief Justice Taney, with reference to the case of Merryman, " If he had never done anything else that was high, heroic and important, his noble vindication of the writ of *habeas corpus* and the dignity and authority of his office against a rash minister of State, who, in the pride of a fancied executive power, came near to the commission of a great crime, will command the admiration and gratitude of every lover of constitutional liberty so long as our institutions shall endure." The crime referred to was the intended imprisonment of the Chief Justice.

Although this crime was not committed, a criminal precedent had been set and was ruthlessly followed. "My lord," said Mr. Seward to Lord Lyons, "I can touch a bell on my right hand and order the imprisonment of a citizen of Ohio; I can touch a bell again and order the imprisonment of a citizen of New York; and no power on earth, except that of the President, can release them. Can the Queen of England do so much ?" When such a power is wielded by any man, or set of men, nothing is left to protect the liberty of the citizen.

On the 24th of May, a Union Convention, consisting of fourteen counties of the State, including the city of Baltimore, and leaving eight unrepresented, met in the city. The counties not represented were Washington, Montgomery, Prince George, Charles, St. Mary's, Dorchester, Somerset, and Worcester. The number of members does not appear to have been large, but it included the names of gentlemen well known and highly respected. The Convention adopted Resolutions which declared, among other things, that the revolution on the part of eleven States was without excuse or palliation, and that the redress of actual or supposed wrongs in connection with the slavery question formed no part of their views or purposes; that the people of this State were unalterably determined to defend the Government of the United States, and would support the Government in all legal and constitutional measures which might be necessary to resist the revolutionists; that the intimations made by the majority of the Legislature at its late session—that the people were humiliated or subjugated by the action of the Government—were gratuitous insults to that people; that the dignity of the State of Maryland, involved in a precise, persistent and effective recognition of all her rights, privileges and immunities under the Constitution of the United States, will be vindicated at all times and under all circumstances by those of her sons who are sincere in their fealty to her and the Government of the Union of which she is part, and to popular constitutional liberty; that while they concurred with the present Executive of the United States that the unity and integrity of the National Union must be preserved, their view of the nature and true principles of the Constitution, of the powers which it confers, and of the duties which it enjoins, and the rights which it secures, as it relates to and affects the question of slavery in many of the essential bearings, is directly opposed to the views of the Executive; that they are fixed in their conviction, amongst others, that a just comprehension of the true principles of the Constitution forbid utterly the formation of political parties on the foundation of the slavery question, and that the Union men will oppose to the utmost of their ability all attempts of the Federal Executive to commingle in any manner its peculiar views on the slavery question with that of maintaining the just powers of the Government.

These resolutions are important as showing the stand taken by a large portion of the Union party of the State in regard to any interference, as the result of the war or otherwise, by the General Government with the provisions of the Constitution with regard to slavery.

After the writ of *habeas corpus* had been thus suspended, martial law, as a consequence, rapidly became all-powerful, and it continued in force during the war. That law is by Judge Black, in his argument before the Supreme Court in the case of *ex parte* Milligan,[1] shown to be simply the rule of irresponsible force. Law becomes helpless before it. *Inter arma silent leges.*

On May 25, 1862, Judge Carmichael, an honored magistrate, while sitting in his court in Easton, was, by the provost marshal and his deputies, assisted by a body of military sent from Baltimore, beaten, and dragged bleeding from the bench, and then imprisoned, because he had on a previous occasion delivered a charge to the grand jury directing them to inquire into certain illegal acts and to indict the offenders. His imprisonment in Forts McHenry, Lafayette, and Delaware, lasted more than six months. On December 4, 1862, he was

---

[1] 4 Wallace Sup. Court R. 2.

unconditionally released, no trial having been granted him, nor any charges made against him. On June 28, 1862, Judge Bartol, of the Court of Appeals of Maryland, was arrested and confined in Fort McHenry. He was released after a few days, without any charge being preferred against him, or any explanation given.

Spies and informers abounded. A rigid supervision was established. Disloyalty, so called, of any kind was a punishable offense. Rebel colors, the red and white, were prohibited. They were not allowed to appear in shop-windows or on children's garments, or anywhere that might offend the Union sentiment. If a newspaper promulgated disloyal sentiments, the paper was suppressed and the editor imprisoned. If a clergyman was disloyal in prayer or sermon, or if he failed to utter a prescribed prayer, he was liable to be treated in the same manner, and was sometimes so treated. A learned and eloquent Lutheran clergyman came to me for advice because he had been summoned before the provost marshal for saying that a nation which incurred a heavy debt in the prosecution of war laid violent hands on the harvests of the future; but his offense was condoned, because it appeared that he had referred to the " Thirty Years' War " and had made no direct reference to the debt of the United States, and perhaps for a better reason—that he had strong Republican friends among his congregation.

If horses and fodder, fences and timber, or houses and land, were taken for the use of the Army, the owner was not entitled to compensation unless he could prove that he was a loyal man; and the proof was required to be furnished through some well-known loyal person, who, of course, was usually paid for his services. Very soon no one was allowed to vote unless he was a loyal man, and soldiers at the polls assisted in settling the question of loyalty.

Nearly all who approved of the war regarded these things as an inevitable military necessity; but those who disapproved deeply resented them as unwarrantable violations of sacred constitutional rights. The consequence was that friendships were dissolved, the ties of blood severed, and an invisible but well-understood line divided the people. The bitterness and even the common mention of these acts have long since ceased, but the tradition survives and still continues to be a factor, silent, but not without influence, in the politics of the State.

History repeats itself. There were deeds done on both sides which bring to mind the wars of England and Scotland and the border strife between those countries. There were flittings to and fro, and adventures and hairbreadth escapes innumerable. Soldiers returned to visit their homes at the risk of their necks. Contraband of every description, and letters and newspapers, found their way across the border. The military lines were long and tortuous, and vulnerable points were not hard to find, and trusty carriers were ready to go anywhere for the love of adventure or the love of gain.

The women were as deeply interested as the men, and were less apprehensive of personal consequences. In different parts of the city, not excepting its stateliest square, where stands the marble column from which the father of his country looked down, sadly as it were, on a divided people, there might have been found, by the initiated, groups of women who, with swift and skillful fingers, were fashioning and making garments strangely various in shape and kind—some for Northern prisons where captives were confined, some for destitute homes beyond the Southern border, in which only women and children were left, and some for Southern camps where ragged soldiers were waiting to be clad.   The work was carried on not without its risks ; but little cared the workers for that.   Perhaps the sensation of danger itself, and a spirit of resistance to an authority which they refused to recognize, gave zest to their toil ; nor did they always think it necessary to inform the good man of the house in which they were assembled either of their presence or of what was going on beneath his roof.

The women who stood by the cause of the Union were not compelled to hide their charitable deeds from the light of day. No need for them to feed and clothe the soldiers of the Union, whose wants were amply supplied by a bountiful Government ; but with untiring zeal they visited the military hospitals on missions of mercy, and when the bloody fields of Antietam and Gettysburg were fought, both they and their Southern sisters hastened, though not with a common purpose, to the aid of the wounded and dying, the victims of civil strife and children of a common country.

CHAPTER VIII.

On the 10th of June, 1861, Major-General Nathaniel P. Banks, of Massachusetts, was appointed in the place of General Cadwallader to the command of the Department of Annapolis, with headquarters at Baltimore. On the 27th of June, General Banks arrested Marshal Kane and confined him in Fort McHenry. He then issued a proclamation announcing that he had superseded Marshal Kane and the commissioners of police, and that he had appointed Colonel John R. Kenly, of the First Regiment of Maryland Volunteers, provost marshal, with the aid and assistance of the subordinate officers of the police department.

The police commissioners, including the mayor, offered no resistance, but adopted and published a resolution declaring that, in the opinion of the board, the forcible suspension of their functions suspended at the same time the active operation of the police law and put the officers and men off duty for the present, leaving them subject, however, to the rules and regulations of the service as to their personal conduct and deportment, and to the orders which the board might see fit thereafter to issue, when the present illegal suspension of their functions should be removed.

The Legislature of Maryland, at its adjourned session on the 22d of June, passed a series of resolutions declaring that the unconstitutional and arbitrary proceedings of the Federal Executive had not been confined to the violation of the personal rights and liberties of the citizens of Maryland, but had been so extended that the property of no man was safe, the sanctity of no dwelling was respected, and that the sacredness of private correspondence no longer existed; that the Senate and House of Delegates of Maryland felt it due to her dignity and independence that history should not record the overthrow of public freedom for an instant within her borders, without recording likewise the indignant expression of her resentment and remonstrance, and they accordingly protested against the oppressive and tyrannical assertion and exercise of military jurisdiction within the limits of Maryland over the persons and property of her citizens by the Government of the United States, and solemnly declared the same to be subversive of the most sacred guarantees of the Constitution, and in flagrant violation of the fundamental and most cherished principles of American free government.

On the first of July, the police commissioners were arrested and imprisoned by order of General Banks, on the ground, as he alleged in a proclamation, that the commissioners had refused to obey his decrees, or to recognize his appointees, and that they continued to hold the police force for some purpose not known to the Government.

General Banks does not say what authority he had to make decrees, or what the decrees were which the commissioners had refused to obey; and as on the 27th of June he had imprisoned the marshal of police, and had put a provost marshal in his place, retaining only the subordinate officers of the police department, and had appointed instead of the men another body of police, all under the control of the provost marshal; and as the commissioners had no right to discharge the police force established by a law of the State, and were left with no duties in relation to the police which they could perform, it is very plain that, whatever motive General Banks may have had for the arrest and imprisonment of the commissioners, it is not stated in his proclamation.

One of the commissioners, Charles D. Hinks, was soon released in consequence of failing health.

On the day of the arrest of the police commissioners the city was occupied by troops, who in large detachments, infantry and artillery, took up positions in Monument Square, Exchange Place, at Camden-street Station and other points, and they mounted guard and bivouacked in the streets for more than a week.

On July 18th, the police commissioners presented to Congress a memorial in which they protested very vigorously against their unlawful arrest and imprisonment.

On the 23d day of July, 1861, the mayor and city council of Baltimore addressed a memorial to the Senate and House of Representatives of the United States, in which, after describing the condition of affairs in Baltimore, they respectfully, yet most earnestly, demanded, as matter of right, that their city might be governed according to the Constitution and laws of the United States and of the State of Maryland, that the citizens might be secure in their persons, houses, papers and effects against unreasonable searches and seizures; that they should not be deprived of life, liberty or property without due process of law; that the military should render obedience to the civil authority; that the municipal laws should be respected, the officers released from imprisonment and restored to the lawful exercise of their functions, and that the police government established by law should be no longer impeded by armed force to the injury of peace and order.   It is perhaps needless to add that the memorial met with no favor.

On the 7th of August, 1861, the Legislature of the State, in a series of resolutions, denounced these proceedings in all their parts, pronouncing them, so far as they affected individuals, a gross and unconstitutional abuse of power which nothing could palliate or excuse, and, in their bearing upon the authority and constitutional powers and privileges of the State herself, a revolutionary subversion of the Federal compact.

The Legislature then adjourned, to meet on the 17th of September.

On the 24th of July, 1861, General Dix had been placed in command of the Department, with his headquarters in Baltimore.   On that day he wrote from Fort McHenry to the Assistant Adjutant-General for re-enforcement of the troops under his command.   He said that there ought to be ten thousand men at Baltimore and Annapolis, and that he could not venture to respond for the quietude of the Department with a smaller number.   At Fort McHenry, as told by his biographer, he exhibited to some ladies of secession proclivities an immense columbiad, and informed them that it was pointed to Monument Square, and if there was an uprising that this piece would be the first he would fire.   But the guns of Fort McHenry were not sufficient.   He built on the east of the city a very strong work, which he called Fort Marshall, and he strengthened the earthwork on Federal

Hill, in the southern part, so that the city lay under the guns of three powerful forts, with several smaller ones. Not satisfied with this, on the 15th of September, 1862, General Dix, after he had been transferred to another department, wrote to Major-General Halleck, then Commander-in-Chief, advising that the ground on which the earthwork on Federal Hill had been erected should be purchased at a cost of one hundred thousand dollars, and that it should be permanently fortified at an additional expense of $250,000. He was of opinion that although the great body of the people were, as he described them, eminently distinguished for their moral virtues, Baltimore had always contained a mass of inflammable material, which would ignite on the slightest provocation. He added that "Fort Federal Hill completely commanded the city, and is capable, from its proximity to the principal business quarters, of assailing any one without injury to the others. The hill seems to have been placed there by Nature as a site for a permanent citadel, and I beg to suggest whether a neglect to appropriate it to its obvious design would not be an unpardonable dereliction of duty."

These views were perhaps extreme even for a major-general commanding in Baltimore, especially as by this time the disorderly element which infests all cities had gone over to the stronger side, and was engaged in the pious work of persecuting rebels. General Halleck, even after this solemn warning, left Federal Hill to the protection of its earthwork.

The opinion which General Dix had of Baltimore extended, though in a less degree, to a large portion of the State, and was shared, in part at least, not only by the other military commanders, but by the Government at Washington.

On the 11th of September, 1861, Simon Cameron, Secre-

tary of War, wrote the following letter to Major-General
Banks, who was at this time in command of a division in
Maryland:

"WAR DEPARTMENT, *September* 11, 1861.

"*General :*—The passage of any act of secession by the Legislature of
Maryland must be prevented. If necessary, all or any part of the members must be arrested. Exercise your own judgment as to the time and
manner, but do the work effectively."

On the 12th of September, Major-General McClellan,
Commander-in-Chief of the Army of the Potomac, wrote a
confidential letter to General Banks reciting that "after full
consultation with the President, Secretary of State, War, etc.,
it has been decided to effect the operation proposed for the
17th." The 17th was the day fixed for the meeting of the
General Assembly, and the operation to be performed was
the arrest of some thirty members of that body, and other
persons besides. Arrangements had been made to have a
Government steamer at Annapolis to receive the prisoners
and convey them to their destination. The plan was to be
arranged with General Dix and Governor Seward, and the
letter closes with leaving this exceedingly important affair to
the tact and discretion of General Banks, and impressing on
him the absolute necessity of secrecy and success.

Accordingly, a number of the most prominent members of
the Legislature, myself, as mayor of Baltimore, and editors
of newspapers, and other citizens, were arrested at midnight.
I was arrested at my country home, near the Relay House
on the Baltimore and Ohio Railroad, by four policemen and
a guard of soldiers. The soldiers were placed in both front
and rear of the house, while the police rapped violently on
the front door. I had gone to bed, but was still awake, for
I had some apprehension of danger. I immediately arose,

render it no service, cannot fail by creating widespread dissatisfaction to disturb the quietude of the city, which I am most anxious to preserve.

" I feel assured that the payment would have been voluntarily discontinued by yourself, as a violation of the principle on which all compensation is bestowed—as a remuneration for an equivalent service actually performed —had you not considered yourself bound by existing laws to make it.

" This order will relieve you from the embarrassment, and I do not doubt that it will be complied with.

" I am, very respectfully,

" Your obedient servant,

" JOHN A. DIX,

" *Major-General Commanding.*"

" MAYOR'S OFFICE, CITY HALL,

" BALTIMORE, *September* 5, 1861.

" Major-General JOHN A. DIX, *Baltimore, Md.*

" *Sir:*—I was not in town yesterday, and did not receive until this morning your letter of the 3d inst. ordering that no further payment be made to the members of the city police.

" The payments have been made heretofore in pursuance of the laws of the State, under the advice of the City Counsellor, by the Register, the Comptroller and myself.

" Without entering into a discussion of the considerations which you have deemed sufficient to justify this proceeding, I feel it to be my duty to enter my protest against this interference, by military authority, with the exercise of powers lawfully committed by the State of Maryland to the officers of the city corporation ; but it is nevertheless not the intention of the city authorities to offer resistance to the order which you have issued, and I shall therefore give public notice to the officers and men of the city police that no further payments may be expected by them.

" There is an arrearage of pay of two weeks due to the force, and the men have by the law and rules of the board been prevented from engaging in any other business or occupation. Most of them have families, who are entirely dependent for support on the pay received.

" I do not understand your order as meaning to prohibit the payment of this arrearage, and shall therefore proceed to make it, unless prevented by your further order.

" I am, very respectfully,

" Your obedient servant,

" GEO. WM. BROWN,

" *Mayor of Baltimore.*"

" HEADQUARTERS DEPARTMENT OF PENNSYLVANIA,
" BALTIMORE, MD., *September* 9, 1861.

" Hon. GEO. WM. BROWN, *Mayor of the City of Baltimore.*

" *Sir :*—Your letter of the 5th inst. was duly received. I cannot, without acquiescing in the violation of a principle, assent to the payment of an arrearage to the members of the old city police, as suggested in the closing paragraph of your letter.

" It was the intention of my letter to prohibit any payment to them subsequently to the day on which it was written.

" You will please, therefore, to consider this as the 'further order' referred to by you.

" I am, very respectfully,

" Your obedient servant,

" JOHN A. DIX,
" *Major-General Commanding.*"

" MAYOR'S OFFICE, CITY HALL,
" BALTIMORE, *September* 11, 1861.

" Major-General JOHN A. DIX, *Baltimore.*

" *Sir :*—I did not come to town yesterday until the afternoon, and then ascertained that my letters had been sent out to my country residence, where, on my return last evening, I found yours of the 9th, in reply to mine of the 5th instant, awaiting me. It had been left at the mayor's office yesterday morning.

" Before leaving the mayor's office, about three o'clock P. M. on the 9th instant, and not having received any reply from you, I had signed a check for the payment of arrears due the police, and the money was on the same day drawn out of the bank and handed over to the proper officers, and nearly the entire amount was by them paid to the police force before the receipt of your letter.

" The suggestion in your letter as to the ' violation of a principle ' requires me to add that I recognize in the action of the Government of the United States in the matter in question nothing but the assertion of superior force.

" Out of regard to the great interests committed to my charge as chief magistrate of the city, I have yielded to that force, and do not feel it necessary to enter into any discussion of the principles upon which the Government sees fit to exercise it.

" Very respectfully,

" Your obedient servant,

" GEO. WM. BROWN,
" *Mayor.*"

The reasons which General Dix assigned for prohibiting me from paying the arrearages due the police present a curious combination. First, there were reasons of State; next, the respect due to the Government; third, his concern for the taxpayers of Baltimore; fourth, the danger to the quiet of the city which he apprehended might arise from the payment; and, finally, there was a principle which he must protect from violation, but what that principle was he did not state.

A striking commentary on these reasons was furnished on the 11th of December, 1863, by a decision of the Court of Appeals of Maryland in the case of the Mayor, etc., of Baltimore *vs.* Charles Howard and others, reported in 20th Maryland Rep., p. 335. The question was whether the interference by the Government of the United States with the Board of Police and police force established by law in the city of Baltimore was without authority of law and did in any manner affect or impair the rights or invalidate the acts of the board. The court held that, though the board was displaced by a force to which they yielded and could not resist, their power and rights under their organization were still preserved, and that they were amenable for any dereliction of official duty, except in so far as they were excused by uncontrollable events. And the court decided that Mr. Hinks, one of the police commissioners, whose case was alone before the court, was entitled to his salary, which had accrued after the board was so displaced.

Subsequently, after the close of the war, the Legislature of the State passed an act for the payment of all arrearages due to the men of the police subsequent to their displacement by the Government of the United States and until their discharge by the Government of the State.

It will be perceived that General Dix delayed replying to my letter of the 5th of September until the 9th; that his reply was not left at the mayor's office until the tenth, and that in the meantime, on the afternoon of the 9th, after waiting for his reply for four days, I paid the arrears due the police, as I had good reason to suppose he intended I should.

A friend of mine, a lawyer of Baltimore, and a pronounced Union man, has, since then, informed me that General Dix showed him my letter of the 5th before my arrest; that my friend asked him whether he had replied to it, and the General replied he had not. My friend answered that he thought a reply was due to me. From all this it does not seem uncharitable to believe that the purpose of General Dix was to put me in the false position of appearing to disobey his order and thus to furnish an excuse for my imprisonment. This lasted until the 27th of November, 1862, a short time after my term of office had expired, when there was a sudden and unexpected release of all the State prisoners in Fort Warren, where we were then confined.

On the 26th of November, 1862, Colonel Justin Dimick, commanding at Fort Warren, received the following telegraphic order from the Adjutant-General's Office, Washington: " The Secretary of War directs that you release all the Maryland State prisoners, also any other State prisoners that may be in your custody, and report to this office."

In pursuance of this order, Colonel Dimick on the following day released from Fort Warren the following State prisoners, without imposing any condition upon them whatever: Severn Teackle Wallis, Henry M. Warfield, William G. Harrison, T. Parkin Scott, ex-members of the Maryland Legislature from Baltimore; George William Brown, ex-Mayor of Baltimore; Charles Howard and William H.

Gatchell, ex-Police Commissioners; George P. Kane, ex-Marshal of Police; Frank Key Howard, one of the editors of the Baltimore *Exchange;* Thomas W. Hall, editor of the Baltimore *South;* Robert Hull, merchant, of Baltimore; Dr. Charles Macgill, of Hagerstown; William H. Winder, of Philadelphia; and B. L. Cutter, of Massachusetts.

General Wool, then in command in Baltimore, issued an order declaring that thereafter no person should be arrested within the limits of the Department except by his order, and in all such cases the charges against the accused party were to be sworn to before a justice of the peace.

As it was intimated that these gentlemen had entered into some engagement as the condition of their release, Mr. Wallis, while in New York on his return home, took occasion to address a letter on the subject to the editor of the New York *World,* in which he said: " No condition whatever was sought to be imposed, and none would have been accepted, as the Secretary of War well knew. Speaking of my fellow-prisoners from Maryland, I have a right to say that they maintained to the last the principle which they asserted from the first—namely, that, if charged with crime, they were entitled to be charged, held and tried in due form of law and not otherwise; and that, in the absence of lawful accusation and process, it was their right to be discharged without terms or conditions of any sort, and they would submit to none."

Many of our fellow-prisoners were from necessity not able to take this stand. There were no charges against them, but there were imperative duties which required their presence at home, and when the Government at Washington adopted the policy of offering liberty to those who would consent to take an oath of allegiance prepared for the occasion, they had been compelled to accept it.

Before this, in December, 1861, the Government at Washington, on application of friends, had granted me a parole for thirty days, that I might attend to some important private business, and for that time I stayed with kind relatives, under the terms of the parole, in Boston.

The following correspondence, which then took place, will show the position which I maintained:

" Boston, January 4, 1862.

" Marshal Keys, *Boston.*

" *Sir :*—I called twice to see you during this week, and in your absence had an understanding with your deputy that I was to surrender myself to you this morning, on the expiration of my parole, in time to be conveyed to Fort Warren, and I have accordingly done so.

" As you have not received any instructions from Washington in regard to the course to be pursued with me, I shall consider myself in your custody until you have had ample time to write to Washington and obtain a reply.

" I desire it, however, to be expressly understood that no further extension of my parole is asked for, or would be accepted at this time.

" It is my right and my wish to return to Baltimore, to resume the performance of my official and private duties.   Respectfully,

" Geo. Wm. Brown."

" Department of State,

" Washington, January 6, 1862.

" John S. Keys, Esq., U. S. Marshal, *Boston.*

" *Sir :*—Your letter of the 4th inst., relative to George W. Brown, has been received.

" In reply, I have to inform you that, if he desires it, you may extend his parole to the period of thirty days. If not, you will please recommit him to Fort Warren and report to this Department.

" I am, sir, very respectfully,

" Your obedient servant,

" F. W. Seward,

" Acting Secretary of State."

" Boston, January 10, 1862.

" Marshal Keys, *Boston.*

" *Sir :*—In my note to you of the 4th inst. I stated that I did not desire a renewal of my parole, but that it was my right and wish to return to Baltimore, to resume the performance of my private and official duties.

"My note was, in substance, as you informed me, forwarded to Hon. W. H. Seward, Secretary of State, in a letter from you to him.

"In reply to your communication, F. W. Seward, Acting Secretary of State, wrote to you under date of the 6th inst. that ' you may extend the parole of George W. Brown if he desires it, but if not, you are directed to recommit him to Fort Warren.'

" It was hardly necessary to give me the option of an extension of parole which I had previously declined, but the offer renders it proper for me to say that the parole was applied for by my friends, to enable me to attend to important private business, affecting the interests of others as well as myself ; that the necessities growing out of this particular matter of business no longer exist, and that I cannot consistently with my ideas of propriety, by accepting a renewal of the parole, place myself in the position of seeming to acquiesce in a prolonged and illegal banishment from my home and duties.   Respectfully,

"GEO. WM. BROWN."

On the 11th of January, 1862, I returned to Fort Warren, and on the 14th an offer was made to renew and extend my parole to ninety days upon condition that I would not pass south of Hudson River. This offer I declined. My term of office expired on the 12th of November, 1862, and soon afterwards I was released, as I have just stated.

It is not my purpose to enter into an account of the trials and hardships of prison-life in the crowded forts in which we were successively confined under strict and sometimes very harsh military rule, but it is due to the memory of the commander at Fort Warren, Colonel Justin Dimick, that I should leave on record the warm feelings of respect and friendship with which he was regarded by the prisoners who knew him best, for the unvarying kindness and humanity with which he performed the difficult and painful duties of his office. As far as he was permitted to do so, he promoted the comfort and convenience of all, and after the war was over and he had been advanced to the rank of General, he came to Baltimore as the honored guest of one of his former prisoners, and while there received the warm and hearty greeting of others of his prisoners who still survived.

CHAPTER IX.

A PERSONAL CHAPTER.

I have now completed my task; but perhaps it will be expected that I should clearly define my own position. I have no objection to do so.

Both from feeling and on principle I had always been opposed to slavery—the result in part of the teaching and example of my parents, and confirmed by my own reading and observation. In early manhood I became prominent in defending the rights of the free colored people of Maryland. In the year 1846 I was associated with a small number of persons, of whom the Rev. William F. Brand, author of the "Life of Bishop Whittingham," and myself, are the only survivors. The other members of the association were Dr. Richard S. Steuart, for many years President of the Maryland Hospital for the Insane, and himself a slaveholder; Galloway Cheston, a merchant and afterwards President of the Board of Trustees of the Johns Hopkins University; Frederick W. Brune, my brother-in-law and law-partner; and Ramsay McHenry, planter. We were preparing to initiate a movement tending to a gradual emancipation within the State, but the growing hostility between the North and the South rendered the plan wholly impracticable, and it was abandoned.

My opinions, however, did not lead me into sympathy with the abolition party. I knew that slavery had existed almost everywhere in the world, and still existed in some places, and that, whatever might be its character elsewhere, it was not in the Southern States "the sum of all villainy." On the contrary, it had assisted materially in the development of the race. Nowhere else, I believe, had negro slaves been so well treated, on the whole, and had advanced so far in civilization. They had learned the necessity, as well as the habit, of labor; the importance—to some extent at least—of thrift; the essential distinctions between right and wrong, and the inevitable difference to the individual between right-doing and wrong-doing; the duty of obedience to law; and—not least —some conception, dim though it might be, of the inspiring teachings of the Christian religion. They had learned also to cherish a feeling of respect and good will towards the best portion of the white race, to whom they looked up, and whom they imitated.

I refused to enlist in a crusade against slavery, not only on constitutional grounds, but for other reasons. If the slaves were freed and clothed with the right of suffrage, they would be incapable of using it properly. If the suffrage were withheld, they would be subjected to the oppression of the white race without the protection afforded by their masters. Thus I could see no prospect of maintaining harmony without a disastrous change in our form of government such as prevailed after the war, in what is called the period of reconstruction. If there were entire equality, and an intermingling of the two races, it would not, as it seemed to me, be for the benefit of either. I knew how strong are race prejudices, especially when stimulated by competition and interest; how cruelly the foreigners, as they were called, had been treated by the people in California, and the Indians by our people everywhere; and how, in my own city, citizens were for years ruthlessly deprived by the Know-Nothing party of the right of suffrage, some because they were of foreign birth, and some because they were Catholics. The problem of slavery was to me a Gordian knot which I knew not how to untie, and which I dared not attempt to cut with the sword. Such a severance involved the horrors of civil war, with the wickedness and demoralization which were sure to follow.

I was deeply attached to the Union from a feeling imbibed in early childhood and constantly strengthened by knowledge and personal experience. I did not believe in secession as a constitutional right, and in Maryland there was no sufficient ground for revolution. It was clearly for her interest to remain in the Union and to free her slaves. An attempt to secede or to revolt would have been an act of folly which I deprecated, although I did believe that she, in common with the rest of the South, had constitutional rights in regard to slavery which the North was not willing to respect.

It was my opinion that the Confederacy would prove to be a rope of sand. I thought that the seceding States should have been allowed to depart in peace, as General Scott advised, and I believed that afterwards the necessities of the situation and their own interest would induce them to return, severally, perhaps, to the old Union, but with slavery peacefully abolished; for, in the nature of things, I knew that slavery could not last forever.

Whether or not my opinions were sound and my hopes well founded, is now a matter of little importance, even to myself, but they were at least sincere and were not concealed.

There can be no true union in a Republic unless the parts are held together by a feeling of common interest, and also of mutual respect.

That there is a common interest no reasonable person can

doubt; but this is not sufficient; and, happily, there is a solid basis for mutual respect also.

I have already stated the grounds on which, from their point of view, the Southern people were justified in their revolt, and even in the midst of the war I recognized what the South is gradually coming to recognize—that the grounds on which the Northern people waged war—love of the Union and hatred of slavery—were also entitled to respect.

I believe that the results achieved—namely, the preservation of the Union and the abolition of slavery—are worth all they have cost.

And yet I feel that I am living in a different land from that in which I was born, and under a different Constitution, and that new perils have arisen sufficient to cause great anxiety. Some of these are the consequences of the war, and some are due to other causes. But every generation must encounter its own trials, and should extract benefit from them if it can. The grave problems growing out of emancipation seem to have found a solution in an improving education of the whole people. Perhaps education is the true means of escape from the other perils to which I have alluded.

Let me state them as they appear to me to exist.

Vast fortunes, which astonish the world, have suddenly been acquired, very many by methods of more than doubtful honesty, while the fortunes themselves are so used as to benefit neither the possessors nor the country.

Republican simplicity has ceased to be a reality, except where it exists as a survival in rural districts, and is hardly now mentioned even as a phrase. It has been superseded by republican luxury and ostentation. The mass of the people, who cannot afford to indulge in either, are sorely tempted to covet both.

The individual man does not rely, as he formerly did, on his own strength and manhood. Organization for a common purpose is resorted to wherever organization is possible. Combinations of capital or of labor, ruled by a few individuals, bestride the land with immense power both for good and evil. In these combinations the individual counts for little, and is but little concerned about his own moral responsibility.

When De Tocqueville, in 1838, wrote his remarkable book on Democracy in America, he expressed his surprise to observe how every public question was submitted to the decision of the people, and that, when the people had decided, the question was settled. Now politicians care little about the opinions of the people, because the people care little about opinions. Bosses have come into existence to ply their vile trade of office-brokerage. Rings are formed in which the bosses are masters and the voters their henchmen. Formerly decent people could not be bought either with money or offices. Political parties have always some honest foundation, but rings are factions like those of Rome in her decline, having no foundation but public plunder.

Communism, socialism, and labor strikes have taken the place of slavery agitation. Many people have come to believe that this is a paternal Government from which they have a right to ask for favors, and not a Republic in which all are equal. Hence States, cities, corporations, individuals, and especially certain favored classes, have no scruple in getting money somehow or other, directly or indirectly, out of the purse of the Nation, as if the Nation had either purse or property which does not belong to the people, for the benefit of the whole people, without favor or partiality towards any.

In many ways there is a dangerous tendency towards the centralization of power in the National Government, with little opposition on the part of the people.

Paper money is held by the Supreme Court to be a lawful substitute for gold and silver coin, partly on the ground that this is the prerogative of European governments.[1] This is strange constitutional doctrine to those who were brought up in the school of Marshall, Story, and Chancellor Kent.

The administration of cities has grown more and more extravagant and corrupt, thus leading to the creation of immense debts which oppress the people and threaten to become unmanageable.

The national Congress, instead of faithfully administering its trust, has become reckless and wasteful of the public money.

But, notwithstanding all this, I rejoice to believe that there is a reserve of power in the American people which has never yet failed to redress great wrongs when they have come to be fully recognized and understood.

A striking instance of this is to be found in the temperance movement, which, extreme as it may be in some respects, shows that the conscience of the entire country is aroused on a subject of vast difficulty and importance.

And other auspicious signs exist, the chief of which I think are that a new zeal is manifested in the cause of education; that people of all creeds come together as they never did before to help in good works; that an independent press, bent on enlightening, not deceiving, the people, is making itself heard and respected; and that younger men, who represent the best hopes and aspirations of the time, are pressing forward to take the place of the politicians of a different school, who represent chiefly their own selfish interests, or else a period of hate and discord which has passed away forever.

These considerations give me hope and confidence in the country as it exists to-day.

---

[1] Legal Tender Case, Vol. 110 U. S. Reports, p. 421.

Baltimore is the place of my birth, of my home, and of my affections. No one could be bound to his native city by ties stronger than mine. Perhaps, in view of the incidents of the past, as detailed in this volume, I may be permitted to express to the good people of Baltimore my sincere and profound gratitude for the generous and unsolicited confidence which, on different occasions, they have reposed in me, and for their good will and kind feeling, which have never been withdrawn during the years, now not a few, which I have spent in their service.

APPENDIX I.

The following account of the alleged conspiracy to assassinate Abraham Lincoln on his journey to Baltimore is taken from the "Life of Abraham Lincoln," by Ward H. Lamon, pp. 511–526:

"Whilst Mr. Lincoln, in the midst of his suite and attendants, was being borne in triumph through the streets of Philadelphia, and a countless multitude of people were shouting themselves hoarse, and jostling and crushing each other around his carriage-wheels, Mr. Felton, the President of the Philadelphia, Wilmington and Baltimore Railway, was engaged with a private detective discussing the details of an alleged conspiracy to murder him at Baltimore. Some months before, Mr. Felton, apprehending danger to the bridges along his line, had taken this man into his pay and sent him to Baltimore to spy out and report any plot that might be found for their destruction. Taking with him a couple of other men and a woman, the detective went about his business with the zeal which necessarily marks his peculiar profession. He set up as a stock-broker, under an assumed name, opened an office, and became a vehement secessionist. His agents were instructed to act with the duplicity which such men generally use; to be rabid on the subject of 'Southern Rights'; to suggest all manner of crimes in vindication of them; and if, by these arts, corresponding sentiments should be elicited from their victims, the 'job' might be considered as prospering. Of course they readily found out what everybody else knew—that Maryland was in a state of great alarm; that her people were forming military associations, and that Governor Hicks was doing his utmost to furnish them with arms, on condition that the arms, in case of need, should be turned against the Federal Government. Whether they detected any plan to burn bridges or not, the chief detective does not relate; but it appears that he soon deserted that inquiry and got, or pretended to get, upon a scent that promised a heavier reward. Being intensely ambitious to shine in the professional way, and something of a politician besides, it struck him that it would be a particularly fine thing to discover a dreadful plot to assassinate the President-elect, and he discovered it accordingly. It was easy to get that far; to furnish tangible proofs of an imaginary conspiracy was a more difficult matter. But Baltimore was seething with political excitement; numerous strangers from the far South crowded its hotels and boarding-houses; great numbers of mechanics and laborers out of employment encumbered its streets; and everywhere politicians, merchants, mechanics, laborers and loafers were engaged in heated discussions about the anticipated war, and the probability of Northern troops being marched through Maryland to slaughter and pillage beyond the Potomac. It would seem like an easy thing to beguile a few individuals of this angry and excited multitude into the expression of some criminal desire; and the opportunity was not wholly lost, although the limited success of the detective under such favorable circumstances is absolutely wonderful. He put his 'shadows' upon several persons whom it suited his pleasure to suspect, and the 'shadows' pursued their work with the keen zest and the cool treachery of their kind. They reported daily to their chief in writing, as he reported in turn to his employer. These documents are neither edifying nor useful: they prove nothing but the baseness of the vocation which gave them existence. They were furnished to Mr. Herndon in full, under the impression that partisan feeling had extinguished in him the love of truth and the obligations of candor, as it had in many writers who preceded him on the same subject-matter. They have been carefully and thoroughly read, analyzed, examined and compared, with an earnest and conscientious desire to discover the truth, if, perchance, any trace of truth might be in them. The process of investigation began with a strong bias in favor of the conclusion at which the detective had arrived. For ten years the author implicitly believed in the reality of the atrocious plot which these spies were supposed to have detected and thwarted; and for ten years he had pleased himself with the reflection that he also had done something to defeat the bloody purpose of the assassins. It was a conviction which could scarcely have been overthrown by evidence less powerful than the detective's weak and contradictory account of his own case. In that account there is literally nothing to sustain the accusation, and much to rebut it. It is perfectly manifest that there was no conspiracy—no conspiracy of a hundred, of fifty, of twenty, of three—no definite purpose in the heart of even one man to murder Mr. Lincoln at Baltimore.

" The reports are all in the form of personal narratives, and for the most relate when the spies went to bed, when they rose, where they ate, what saloons and brothels they visited, and what blackguards they met and ' drinked ' with. One of them shadowed a loud-mouthed drinking fellow named Luckett, and another, a poor scapegrace and braggart named Hilliard. These wretches ' drinked ' and talked a great deal, hung about bars, haunted disreputable houses, were constantly half drunk, and easily excited to use big and threatening words by the faithless protestations and cunning management of the spies. Thus Hilliard was made to say that he thought a man who should act the part of Brutus in these times would deserve well of his country; and Luckett was induced to declare that he knew a man who would kill Lincoln. At length the great arch-conspirator—the Brutus, the Orsini of the New World, to whom Luckett and Hilliard, the 'national volunteers,' and all such, were as mere puppets —condescended to reveal himself in the most obliging and confiding manner. He made no mystery of his cruel and desperate scheme. He did not guard it as a dangerous secret, or choose his confidants with the circumspection which political criminals, and especially assassins, have generally thought proper to observe. Very many persons knew what he was about, and levied on their friends for small sums— five, ten and twenty dollars—to further the Captain's plan. Even Luckett was deep enough in the awful plot to raise money for it; and when he took one of the spies to a public bar-room and introduced him to the 'Captain,' the latter sat down and talked it all over without the slightest reserve. When was there ever before such a loud-mouthed conspirator, such a trustful and innocent assassin! His name was Ferrandini, his occupation that of a barber, his place of business beneath Barnum's Hotel, where the sign of the bloodthirsty villain still invites the unsuspecting public to come in for a shave.

"'Mr. Luckett,' so the spy relates, 'said that he was not going home this evening; and if I would meet him at Barr's saloon, on South street, he would introduce me to Ferrandini. This was unexpected to me; but I determined to take the chances, and agreed to meet Mr. Luckett at the place named

at 7 P. M.   Mr. Luckett left about 2.30 P. M., and I went
to dinner.

" ' I was at the office in the afternoon in hopes that Mr.
Felton might call, but he did not ; and at 6.15 P. M. I went
to supper.   After supper I went to Barr's saloon, and found
Mr. Luckett and several other gentlemen there.   He asked
me to drink, and introduced me to Captain Ferrandini and
Captain Turner.   He eulogized me very highly as a neighbor
of his, and told Ferrandini that I was the gentleman who
had given the twenty-five dollars he (Luckett) had given to
Ferrandini.

" ' The conversation at once got into politics; and Ferrandini, who is a fine-looking, intelligent-appearing person, became very excited.   He shows the Italian in, I think, a very
marked degree ; and, although excited, yet was cooler than
what I had believed was the general characteristic of Italians.
He has lived South for many years, and is thoroughly imbued
with the idea that the South must rule ; that they (Southern-
ers) have been outraged in their rights by the election of
Lincoln, and freely justified resorting to any means to prevent
Lincoln from taking his seat; and, as he spoke, his eyes
fairly glared and glistened, and his whole frame quivered ;
but he was fully conscious of all he was doing.   He is a man
well calculated for controlling and directing the ardent-
minded ; he is an enthusiast, and believes that, to use his
own words, "murder of any kind is justifiable and right to
save the rights of the Southern people."   In all his views he
was ably seconded by Captain Turner.

" ' Captain Turner is an American; but although very
much of a gentleman, and possessing warm Southern feelings,
he is not by any means so dangerous a man as Ferrandini, as
his ability for exciting others is less powerful; but that he is

a bold and proud man there is no doubt, as also that he is entirely under the control of Ferrandini. In fact, he could not be otherwise, for even I myself felt the influence of this man's strange power; and, wrong though I knew him to be, I felt strangely unable to keep my mind balanced against him.

"'Ferrandini said, "Never, never, shall Lincoln be President!" His life (Ferrandini's) was of no consequence; he was willing to give it up for Lincoln's; he would sell it for that abolitionist's; and as Orsini had given his life for Italy, so was he (Ferrandini) ready to die for his country and the rights of the South; and said Ferrandini, turning to Captain Turner, "We shall all die together: we shall show the North that we fear them not. Every man, Captain," said he, "will on that day prove himself a hero. The first shot fired, the main traitor (Lincoln) dead, and all Maryland will be with us, and the South shall be free; and the North must then be ours. Mr. Hutchins," said Ferrandini, "if I alone must do it, I shall: Lincoln shall die in this city."

"'Whilst we were thus talking, we (Mr. Luckett, Turner, Ferrandini and myself) were alone in one corner of the bar-room, and, while talking, two strangers had got pretty near us. Mr. Luckett called Ferrandini's attention to this, and intimated that they were listening; and we went up to the bar, drinked again at my expense, and again retired to another part of the room, at Ferrandini's request, to see if the strangers would again follow us. Whether by accident or design, they again got near us; but of course we were not talking of any matter of consequence. Ferrandini said he suspected they were spies, and suggested that he had to attend a secret meeting, and was apprehensive that the two strangers might follow him; and, at Mr. Luckett's request,

I remained with him (Luckett) to watch the movements of the strangers. I assured Ferrandini that if they would attempt to follow him, we would whip them.

" ' Ferrandini and Turner left to attend the meeting, and, anxious as I was to follow them myself, I was obliged to remain with Mr. Luckett to watch the strangers, which we did for about fifteen minutes, when Mr. Luckett said that he should go to a friend's to stay over night, and I left for my hotel, arriving there at about 9 P. M., and soon retired.'

" It is in a secret communication between hireling spies and paid informers that these ferocious sentiments are attributed to the poor knight of the soap-pot. No disinterested person would believe the story upon such evidence; and it will appear hereafter that even the detective felt that it was too weak to mention among his strong points, at that decisive moment when he revealed all he knew to the President and his friends. It is probably a mere fiction. If it had had any foundation in fact, we are inclined to believe that the sprightly and eloquent barber would have dangled at a rope's end long since. He would hardly have been left to shave and plot in peace, while the members of the Legislature, the Police Marshal, and numerous private gentlemen, were locked up in Federal prisons. When Mr. Lincoln was actually slain, four years later, and the cupidity of the detectives was excited by enormous rewards, Ferrandini was totally unmolested. But even if Ferrandini really said all that is here imputed to him, he did no more than many others around him were doing at the same time. He drank and talked, and made swelling speeches; but he never took, nor seriously thought of taking, the first step toward the frightful tragedy he is said to have contemplated.

" The detectives are cautious not to include in the supposed plot to murder any person of eminence, power, or influence. Their game is all of the smaller sort, and, as they conceived, easily taken—witless vagabonds like Hilliard and Luckett, and a barber, whose calling indicates his character and associations.[1] They had no fault to find with the Governor of the State; he was rather a lively trimmer, to be sure, and very anxious to turn up at last on the winning side; but it was manifestly impossible that one in such an exalted station could meditate murder. Yet, if they had pushed their inquiries with an honest desire to get at the truth, they might have found much stronger evidence against the Governor than that which they pretend to have found against the barber. In the Governor's case the evidence is documentary, written, authentic—over his own hand, clear and conclusive as pen and ink could make it. As early as the previous November, Governor Hicks had written the following letter; and, notwithstanding its treasonable and murderous import, the writer became conspicuously loyal before spring, and lived to reap splendid rewards and high honors, under the auspices of the Federal Government, as the most patriotic and devoted Union man in Maryland. The person to whom the letter was addressed was equally fortunate; and, instead of drawing out his comrades in the field to 'kill Lincoln and his men,' he was sent to Congress by power exerted from Washington at a time when the administration selected the representatives of Maryland, and performed all his duties right loyally and acceptably. Shall one be taken and another left? Shall Hicks go to the Senate and Webster to Congress,

[1] Mr. Ferrandini, now in advanced years, still lives in Baltimore, and declares the charge of conspiracy to be wholly absurd and fictitious, and those who know him will, I think, believe that he is an unlikely person to be engaged in such a plot.

while the poor barber is held to the silly words which he is
alleged to have sputtered out between drinks in a low grog-
gery, under the blandishments and encouragements of an
eager spy, itching for his reward ?

    " ' STATE OF MARYLAND,
        " ' EXECUTIVE CHAMBER,
           " ' ANNAPOLIS, *November* 9, 1860.
" ' Hon. E. H. WEBSTER.

  " ' *My Dear Sir :*—I have pleasure in acknowledging receipt of your favor
introducing a very clever gentleman to my acquaintance (though a Demo').
I regret to say that we have, at this time, no arms on hand to distribute, but
assure you at the earliest possible moment your company shall have arms ;
they have complied with all required on their part. We have some
delay, in consequence of contracts with Georgia and Alabama ahead of
us. We expect at an early day an additional supply, and of first received
your people shall be furnished. Will they be good men to send out to kill
Lincoln and his men ? If not, suppose the arms would be better sent South.

  " ' How does late election sit with you ? 'Tis too bad. Harford nothing to
reproach herself for.
      " ' Your obedient servant,
          " ' THOS. H. HICKS.'

  " With the Presidential party was Hon. Norman B. Judd ;
he was supposed to exercise unbounded influence over the new
President ; and with him, therefore, the detective opened
communications. At various places along the route Mr.
Judd was given vague hints of the impending danger, accompanied by the usual assurances of the skill and activity of
the patriots who were perilling their lives in a rebel city to
save that of the Chief Magistrate. When he reached New
York, he was met by the woman who had originally gone
with the other spies to Baltimore. She had urgent messages
from her chief—messages that disturbed Mr. Judd exceedingly. The detective was anxious to meet Mr. Judd and the
President, and a meeting was accordingly arranged to take
place at Philadelphia.

" Mr. Lincoln reached Philadelphia on the afternoon of the 21st. The detective had arrived in the morning, and improved the interval to impress and enlist Mr. Felton. In the evening he got Mr. Judd and Mr. Felton into his room at the St. Louis Hotel, and told them all he had learned. He dwelt at large on the fierce temper of the Baltimore secessionists; on the loose talk he had heard about ' fireballs or hand-grenades'; on a ' privateer' said to be moored somewhere in the bay; on the organization called National Volunteers; on the fact that, eavesdropping at Barnum's Hotel, he had overheard Marshal Kane intimate that he would not supply a police force on some undefined occasion, but what the occasion was he did not know. He made much of his miserable victim, Hilliard, whom he held up as a perfect type of the class from which danger was to be apprehended; but concerning " Captain " Ferrandini and his threats, he said, according to his own account, not a single word. He had opened his case, his whole case, and stated it as strongly as he could. Mr. Judd was very much startled, and was sure that it would be extremely imprudent for Mr. Lincoln to pass through Baltimore in open daylight, according to the published programme. But he thought the detective ought to see the President himself; and, as it was wearing toward nine o'clock, there was no time to lose. It was agreed that the part taken by the detective and Mr. Felton should be kept secret from every one but the President. Mr. Sanford, President of the American Telegraph Company, had also been co-operating in the business, and the same stipulation was made with regard to him.

"Mr. Judd went to his own room at the Continental, and the detective followed. The crowd in the hotel was very dense, and it took some time to get a message to Mr. Lincoln.

But it finally reached him, and he responded in person.   Mr. Judd introduced the detective, and the latter told his story over again, with a single variation: this time he mentioned the name of Ferrandini along with Hilliard's, but gave no more prominence to one than to the other.

"Mr. Judd and the detective wanted Lincoln to leave for Washington that night.   This he flatly refused to do.   He had engagements with the people, he said, to raise a flag over Independence Hall in the morning, and to exhibit himself at Harrisburg in the afternoon, and these engagements he would not break in any event.   But he would raise the flag, go to Harrisburg, 'get away quietly' in the evening, and permit himself to be carried to Washington in the way they thought best.   Even this, however, he conceded with great reluctance.   He condescended to cross-examine the detective on some parts of his narrative, but at no time did he seem in the least degree alarmed.   He was earnestly requested not to communicate the change of plan to any member of his party except Mr. Judd, nor permit even a suspicion of it to cross the mind of another.   To this he replied that he would be compelled to tell Mrs. Lincoln, 'and he thought it likely that she would insist upon W. H. Lamon going with him; but, aside from that, no one should know.'

"In the meantime, Mr. Seward had also discovered the conspiracy.   He dispatched his son to Philadelphia to warn the President-elect of the terrible plot into whose meshes he was about to run.   Mr. Lincoln turned him over to Judd, and Judd told him they already knew all about it.   He went away with just enough information to enable his father to anticipate the exact moment of Mr. Lincoln's surreptitious arrival in Washington.

"Early on the morning of the 22d, Mr. Lincoln raised the

flag over Independence Hall, and departed for Harrisburg. On the way Mr. Judd ' gave him a full and precise detail of the arrangements that had been made ' the previous night. After the conference with the detective, Mr. Sanford, Colonel Scott, Mr. Felton, railroad and telegraph officials, had been sent for, and came to Mr. Judd's room. They occupied nearly the whole of the night in perfecting the plan. It was finally understood that about six o'clock the next evening Mr. Lincoln should slip away from the Jones Hotel, at Harrisburg, in company with a single member of his party. A special car and engine would be provided for him on the track outside the depot. All other trains on the road would be 'side-tracked' until this one had passed. Mr. Sanford would forward skilled 'telegraph-climbers,' and see that all the wires leading out of Harrisburg were cut at six o'clock, and kept down until it was known that Mr. Lincoln had reached Washington in safety. The detective would meet Mr. Lincoln at the West Philadelphia Depot with a carriage, and conduct him by a circuitous route to the Philadelphia, Wilmington and Baltimore Depot. Berths for four would be pre-engaged in the sleeping-car attached to the regular midnight train for Baltimore. This train Mr. Felton would cause to be detained until the conductor should receive a package, containing important 'Government dispatches,' addressed to 'E. J. Allen, Willard's Hotel, Washington.' This package was made up of old newspapers, carefully wrapped and sealed, and delivered to the detective to be used as soon as Mr. Lincoln was lodged in the car. Mr. Lincoln approved of the plan, and signified his readiness to acquiesce. Then Mr. Judd, forgetting the secrecy which the spy had so impressively enjoined, told Mr. Lincoln that the step he was about to take was one of such transcendent importance that he thought 'it should be communicated to the other gentlemen of the party.' Mr. Lincoln said, 'You can do as you like about that.' Mr. Judd now changed his seat; and Mr. Nicolay, whose suspicions seem to have been aroused by this mysterious conference, sat down beside him and said: 'Judd, there is something *up*. What is it, if it is proper that I should know?' 'George,' answered Judd, 'there is no necessity for your knowing it. One man can keep a matter better than two.'

"Arrived at Harrisburg, and the public ceremonies and speechmaking over, Mr. Lincoln retired to a private parlor in the Jones House, and Mr. Judd summoned to meet him Judge Davis, Colonel Lamon, Colonel Sumner, Major Hunter and Captain Pope. The three latter were officers of the regular army, and had joined the party after it had left Springfield. Judd began the conference by stating the alleged fact of the Baltimore conspiracy, how it was detected, and how it was proposed to thwart it by a midnight expedition to Washington by way of Philadelphia. It was a great surprise to most of those assembled. Colonel Sumner was the first to break silence. 'That proceeding,' said he, 'will be a damned piece of cowardice.' Mr. Judd considered this a 'pointed hit,' but replied that 'that view of the case had already been presented to Mr. Lincoln.' Then there was a general interchange of opinions, which Sumner interrupted by saying, 'I'll get a squad of cavalry, sir, and *cut* our way to Washington, sir!' 'Probably before that day comes,' said Mr. Judd, 'the inauguration-day will have passed. It is important that Mr. Lincoln should be in Washington that day.' Thus far Judge Davis had expressed no opinion, but 'had put various questions to test the truthfulness of the story.' He now turned to Mr. Lincoln and said, 'You personally heard the detective's story. You have heard this discussion. What is your judgment in the matter?' 'I have listened,' answered Mr. Lincoln, 'to this discussion with interest. I see no reason, no good reason, to change the programme, and I am for carrying it out as arranged by Judd.' There was no longer any dissent as to the plan itself; but one question still remained to be disposed of. Who should accompany the President on his perilous ride? Mr. Judd again took the lead, declaring that he and Mr. Lincoln had previously determined that but one man ought to go, and that Colonel Lamon had been selected as the proper person. To this Sumner violently demurred. '*I* have undertaken,' he exclaimed, 'to see Mr. Lincoln to Washington.'

" Mr. Lincoln was hastily dining when a close carriage was brought to the side door of the hotel. He was called, hurried to his room, changed his coat and hat, and passed rapidly through the hall and out of the door. As he was stepping into the carriage, it became manifest that Sumner was determined to get in also. 'Hurry with him,' whispered Judd to Lamon, and at the same time, placing his hand on Sumner's shoulder, said aloud, 'One moment, Colonel!' Sumner turned around, and in that moment the carriage drove rapidly away. 'A madder man,' says Mr. Judd, 'you never saw.'

" Mr. Lincoln and Colonel Lamon got on board the car without discovery or mishap. Besides themselves, there was no one in or about the car but Mr. Lewis, General Superintendent of the Pennsylvania Central Railroad, and Mr. Franciscus, superintendent of the division over which they were about to pass. As Mr. Lincoln's dress on this occasion has been much discussed, it may be as well to state that he

wore a soft, light felt hat, drawn down over his face when it
seemed necessary or convenient, and a shawl thrown over his
shoulders, and pulled up to assist in disguising his features
when passing to and from the carriage.   This was all there
was of the 'Scotch cap and cloak,' so widely celebrated in
the political literature of the day.

"At ten o'clock they reached Philadelphia, and were met by
the detective and one Mr. Kinney, an under official of the
Philadelphia, Wilmington and Baltimore Railroad.   Lewis
and Franciscus bade Mr. Lincoln adieu.   Mr. Lincoln,
Colonel Lamon and the detective seated themselves in a
carriage which stood in waiting, and Mr. Kinney got upon
the box with the driver.   It was a full hour and a half
before the Baltimore train was to start, and Mr. Kinney
found it necessary 'to consume the time by driving north-
ward in search of some imaginary person.'

"On the way through Philadelphia, Mr. Lincoln told his
companions about the message he had received from Mr.
Seward.   This new discovery was infinitely more appalling
than the other.   Mr. Seward had been informed 'that about
fifteen thousand men were organized to prevent his (Lincoln's)
passage through Baltimore, and that arrangements were made
by these parties *to blow up the railroad track, fire the train,*'
etc.   In view of these unpleasant circumstances, Mr. Seward
recommended a change of route.   Here was a plot big enough
to swallow up the little one, which we are to regard as the
peculiar property of Mr. Felton's detective.   Hilliard, Ferrandini and Luckett disappear among the 'fifteen thousand,'
and their maudlin and impotent twaddle about the 'abolition
tyrant' looks very insignificant beside the bloody massacre,
conflagration and explosion now foreshadowed.

"As the moment for the departure of the Baltimore train

drew near, the carriage paused in the dark shadows of the depot building. It was not considered prudent to approach the entrance. The spy passed in first and was followed by Mr. Lincoln and Colonel Lamon. An agent of the former directed them to the sleeping-car, which they entered by the rear door. Mr. Kinney ran forward and delivered to the conductor the important package prepared for the purpose; and in three minutes the train was in motion. The tickets for the whole party had been procured beforehand. Their berths were ready, but had only been preserved from invasion by the statement that they were retained for a sick man and his attendants. The business had been managed very adroitly by the female spy, who had accompanied her employer from Baltimore to Philadelphia to assist him in this, the most delicate and important affair of his life. Mr. Lincoln got into his bed immediately, and the curtains were drawn together. When the conductor came around, the detective handed him the 'sick man's' ticket, and the rest of the party lay down also. None of 'our party appeared to be sleepy,' says the detective, 'but we all lay quiet, and nothing of importance transpired.' . . . . During the night Mr. Lincoln indulged in a joke or two in an undertone; but, with that exception, the two sections occupied by them were perfectly silent. The detective said he had men stationed at various places along the road to let him know 'if all was right,' and he rose and went to the platform occasionally to observe their signals, but returned each time with a favorable report.

"At thirty minutes after three the train reached Baltimore. One of the spy's assistants came on board and informed him in a whisper that all was right. The woman [the female detective] got out of the car. Mr. Lincoln lay close in his

berth, and in a few moments the car was being slowly drawn
through the quiet streets of the city toward the Washington
Depot.   There again there was another pause, but no sound
more alarming than the noise of shifting cars and engines.
The passengers, tucked away on their narrow shelves, dozed
on as peacefully as if Mr. Lincoln had never been born. . . .

" In due time the train sped out of the suburbs of Baltimore,
and the apprehensions of the President and his friends
diminished with each welcome revolution of the wheels.   At
six o'clock the dome of the Capitol came in sight, and a
moment later they rolled into the long, unsightly building
which forms the Washington Depot.   They passed out of the
car unobstructed, and pushed along with the living stream
of men and women towards the outer door.   One man alone
in the great crowd seemed to watch Mr. Lincoln with special
attention.   Standing a little on one side, he 'looked very
sharp at him,' and, as he passed, seized hold of his hand and
said in a loud tone of voice, 'Abe, you can't play that on
me.'   The detective and Col. Lamon were instantly alarmed.
One of them raised his fist to strike the stranger; but Mr.
Lincoln caught his arm and said, ' Don't strike him! don't
strike him! It is Washburne. Don't you know him ?' Mr.
Seward had given to Mr. Washburne a hint of the information received through his son, and Mr. Washburne knew its
value as well as another.   For the present the detective
admonished him to keep quiet, and they passed on together.
Taking a hack, they drove towards Willard's Hotel.   Mr.
Lincoln, Mr. Washburne and the detective got out into the
street and approached the ladies' entrance, while Col. Lamon
drove on to the main entrance, and sent the proprietor to
meet his distinguished guest at the side door.   A few
minutes later Mr. Seward arrived, and was introduced to the

company by Mr. Washburne. He spoke in very strong terms of the great danger which Mr. Lincoln had so narrowly escaped, and most heartily applauded the wisdom of the 'secret passage.' 'I informed Gov. Seward of the nature of the information I had,' says the detective, 'and that I had no information of any large organization in Baltimore ; but the Governor reiterated that he had conclusive evidence of this.' . . . .

"That same day Mr. Lincoln's family and suite passed through Baltimore on the special train intended for him. They saw no sign of any disposition to burn them alive, or to blow them up with gunpowder, but went their way unmolested and very happy.

"Mr. Lincoln soon learned to regret the midnight ride. His friends reproached him ; his enemies taunted him. He was convinced that he had committed a grave mistake in yielding to the solicitations of a professional spy and of friends too easily alarmed. He saw that he had fled from a danger purely imaginary, and felt the shame and mortification natural to a brave man under such circumstances. But he was not disposed to take all the responsibility to himself, and frequently upbraided the writer for having aided and assisted him to demean himself at the very moment in all his life when his behavior should have exhibited the utmost dignity and composure.

"The news of his surreptitious entry into Washington occasioned much and varied comment throughout the country; but important events followed it in such rapid succession that its real significance was soon lost sight of; enough that Mr. Lincoln was safely at the Capital, and in a few days would in all probability assume the power confided to his hands."

APPENDIX II.

EXTRACT FROM THE OPINION OF THE SUPREME COURT OF
THE UNITED STATES, DELIVERED BY CHIEF JUSTICE TANEY
IN THE CASE OF DRED SCOTT *vs.* SANDFORD, 19 HOW. 407.

"It is difficult at this day to realize the state of public opinion in relation to that unfortunate race" (the African) "which prevailed in the civilized and enlightened portions of the world at the time of the Declaration of Independence, and when the Constitution of the United States was framed and adopted.

"But the public history of every European nation displays it in a manner too plain to be mistaken.

"They had for more than a century before been regarded as beings of an inferior order, and altogether unfit to associate with the white race, either in social or political relations; and so far inferior, that they had no rights which the white man was bound to respect; and that the negro might justly and lawfully be reduced to slavery for his benefit."

APPENDIX III.

Ex parte   } Before the Chief Justice of the Supreme
JOHN MERRYMAN.   } Court of the United States, at Chambers.

The application in this case for a writ of *habeas corpus* is made to me under the fourteenth section of the Judiciary Act of 1789, which renders effectual for the citizen the constitutional privilege of the writ of *habeas corpus*. That act gives to the courts of the United States, as well as to each justice of the Supreme Court and to every district judge, power to grant writs of *habeas corpus* for the purpose of an inquiry into the cause of commitment. The petition was presented to me at Washington, under the impression that I would order the prisoner to be brought before me there; but as he was confined in Fort McHenry, in the city of Baltimore, which is in my circuit, I resolved to hear it in the latter city, as obedience to the writ under such circumstances would not withdraw General Cadwallader, who had him in charge, from the limits of his military command.

The petition presents the following case:

The petitioner resides in Maryland, in Baltimore County. While peaceably in his own house, with his family, it was, at two o'clock on the morning of the 25th of May, 1861, entered by an armed force professing to act under military orders.

He was then compelled to rise from his bed, taken into custody and conveyed to Fort McHenry, where he is imprisoned by the commanding officer, without warrant from any lawful authority.

The commander of the fort, General George Cadwallader, by whom he is detained in confinement, in his return to the writ, does not deny any of the facts alleged in the petition. He states that the prisoner was arrested by order of General Keim, of Pennsylvania, and conducted as aforesaid to Fort McHenry by his order, and placed in his (General Cadwallader's) custody, to be there detained by him as a prisoner.

A copy of the warrant or order under which the prisoner was arrested was demanded by his counsel and refused. And it is not alleged in the return that any specific act, constituting any offense against the laws of the United States, has been charged against him upon oath ; but he appears to have been arrested upon general charges of treason and rebellion, without proof, and without giving the names of the witnesses, or specifying the acts which, in the judgment of the military officer, constituted these crimes. Having the prisoner thus in custody upon these vague and unsupported accusations, he refuses to obey the writ of *habeas corpus*, upon the ground that he is duly authorized by the President to suspend it.

The case, then, is simply this : A military officer, residing in Pennsylvania, issues an order to arrest a citizen of Maryland upon vague and indefinite charges, without any proof, so far as appears. Under this order his house is entered in the night, he is seized as a prisoner and conveyed to Fort McHenry, and there kept in close confinement. And when a *habeas corpus* is served on the commanding officer, requiring him to produce the prisoner before a justice of the Supreme Court, in order that he may examine into the legality of the imprisonment, the answer of the officer is that he is authorized by the President to suspend the writ of *habeas corpus* at his discretion, and, in the exercise of that discretion, suspends it in this case, and on that ground refuses obedience to the writ.

As the case comes before me, therefore, I understand that the President not only claims the right to suspend the writ of *habeas corpus* himself at his discretion, but to delegate that discretionary power to a military officer, and to leave it to him to determine whether he will or will not obey judicial process that may be served upon him.

No official notice has been given to the courts of justice, or to the public, by proclamation or otherwise, that the President claimed this power, and had exercised it in the manner stated in the return. And I certainly listened to it with some surprise; for I had supposed it to be one of those points of constitutional law upon which there was no difference of opinion, and that it was admitted on all hands that the privilege of the writ could not be suspended except by act of Congress.

When the conspiracy of which Aaron Burr was the head became so formidable and was so extensively ramified as to justify, in Mr. Jefferson's opinion, the suspension of the writ, he claimed on his part no power to suspend it, but communicated his opinion to Congress, with all the proofs in his possession, in order that Congress might exercise its discretion upon the subject, and determine whether the public safety required it. And in the debate which took place upon the subject, no one suggested that Mr. Jefferson might exercise the power himself, if, in his opinion, the public safety demanded it.

Having therefore regarded the question as too plain and too

well settled to be open to dispute, if the commanding officer
had stated that upon his own responsibility, and in the exercise of his own discretion, he refused obedience to the writ, I
should have contented myself with referring to the clause in
the Constitution, and to the construction it received from
every jurist and statesman of that day, when the case of Burr
was before them.   But being thus officially notified that the
privilege of the writ has been suspended under the orders
and by the authority of the President, and believing, as I do,
that the President has exercised a power which he does not
possess under the Constitution, a proper respect for the high
office he fills requires me to state plainly and fully the
grounds of my opinion, in order to show that I have not
ventured to question the legality of his act without a careful
and deliberate examination of the whole subject.

The clause of the Constitution which authorizes the suspension of the privilege of the writ of *habeas corpus* is in the
ninth section of the first article.

This article is devoted to the legislative department of the
United States, and has not the slightest reference to the
Executive Department.   It begins by providing "that all
legislative powers therein granted shall be vested in a Congress of the United States, which shall consist of a Senate
and House of Representatives"; and after prescribing the
manner in which these two branches of the legislative department shall be chosen, it proceeds to enumerate specifically
the legislative powers which it thereby grants, and at the
conclusion of this specification a clause is inserted giving
Congress "the power to make all laws which shall be necessary and proper for carrying into execution the foregoing
powers, and all other powers vested by this Constitution in
the Government of the United States, or in any department
or office thereof."

The power of legislation granted by this latter clause is by its words carefully confined to the specific objects before enumerated. But as this limitation was unavoidably somewhat indefinite, it was deemed necessary to guard more effectually certain great cardinal principles essential to the liberty of the citizen, and to the rights and equality of the States, by denying to Congress, in express terms, any power of legislation over them. It was apprehended, it seems, that such legislation might be attempted under the pretext that it was necessary and proper to carry into execution the powers granted; and it was determined that there should be no room to doubt, where rights of such vital importance were concerned, and accordingly this clause is immediately followed by an enumeration of certain subjects to which the powers of legislation shall not extend. The great importance which the framers of the Constitution attached to the privilege of the writ of *habeas corpus* to protect the liberty of the citizen, is proved by the fact that its suspension, except in cases of invasion or rebellion, is first in the list of prohibited powers— and even in these cases the power is denied and its exercise prohibited, unless the public safety shall require it. It is true that in the cases mentioned, Congress is of necessity the judge of whether the public safety does, or does not, require it; and its judgment is conclusive. But the introduction of these words is a standing admonition to the legislative body of the danger of suspending it, and of the extreme caution they should exercise before they give the Government of the United States such power over the liberty of a citizen.

It is the second article of the Constitution that provides for the organization of the Executive Department, and enumerates the powers conferred on it, and prescribes its duties. And if the high power over the liberty of the citizen now claimed was intended to be conferred on the President, it would undoubtedly be found in plain words in this article. But there is not a word in it that can furnish the slightest ground to justify the exercise of the power.

The article begins by declaring that the executive power shall be vested in a President of the United States of America, to hold his office during the term of four years, and then proceeds to prescribe the mode of election, and to specify in precise and plain words the powers delegated to him, and the duties imposed upon him. The short term for which he is elected, and the narrow limits to which his power is confined, show the jealousy and apprehensions of future danger which the framers of the Constitution felt in relation to that department of the Government, and how carefully they withheld from it many of the powers belonging to the Executive Branch of the English Government which were considered as dangerous to the liberty of the subject, and conferred (and that in clear and specific terms) those powers only which were deemed essential to secure the successful operation of the Government.

He is elected, as I have already said, for the brief term of four years, and is made personally responsible by impeachment for malfeasance in office. He is from necessity and the nature of his duties the Commander-in-Chief of the Army and Navy, and of the militia when called into actual service. But no appropriation for the support of the Army can be made by Congress for a longer term than two years, so that it is in the power of the succeeding House of Representatives to withhold the appropriation for its support, and thus disband it, if, in their judgment, the President used or designed to use it for improper purposes. And although the militia, when in actual service, is under his command, yet the appointment of the officers is reserved to the States, as a security against the use of the military power for purposes dangerous to the liberties of the people or the rights of the States.

So, too, his powers in relation to the civil duties and authority necessarily conferred on him are carefully restricted, as well as those belonging to his military character. He cannot appoint the ordinary officers of Government, nor make a treaty with a foreign nation or Indian tribe, without the advice and consent of the Senate, and cannot appoint even inferior officers unless he is authorized by an Act of Congress to do so. He is not empowered to arrest any one charged with an offense against the United States, and whom he may, from the evidence before him, believe to be guilty; nor can he authorize any officer, civil or military, to exercise this power; for the fifth article of the Amendments to the Constitution expressly provides that no person "shall be deprived of life, liberty or property without due process of law"—that is, judicial process. Even if the privilege of the writ of *habeas corpus* were suspended by Act of Congress, and a party not subject to the rules and articles of war were afterwards arrested and imprisoned by regular judicial process, he could not be detained in prison or brought to trial before a military tribunal; for the article in the Amendments to the Constitution immediately following the one above referred to—that is, the sixth article—provides that "in all criminal prosecutions the accused shall enjoy the right to a speedy and public trial by an impartial jury of the State and district wherein the crime shall have been committed, which district shall have been previously ascertained by law; and to be informed of the nature and cause of the accusation; to be confronted with the witnesses against him; to have compulsory process for obtaining witnesses in his favor, and to have the assistance of counsel for his defense."

The only power, therefore, which the President possesses, where the "life, liberty, or property" of a private citizen is concerned, is the power and duty prescribed in the third section of the second article, which requires "that he shall take care that the laws be faithfully executed." He is not authorized to execute them himself, or through agents or officers, civil or military, appointed by himself, but he is to take care that they be faithfully carried into execution as they are expounded and adjudged by the co-ordinate branch of the Government to which that duty is assigned by the Constitution. It is thus made his duty to come in aid of the judicial authority, if it shall be resisted by a force too strong to be overcome without the assistance of the executive arm. But in exercising this power he acts in subordination to judicial authority, assisting it to execute its process and enforce its judgments.

With such provisions in the Constitution, expressed in language too clear to be misunderstood by any one, I can see no ground whatever for supposing that the President, in any emergency or in any state of things, can authorize the suspension of the privilege of the writ of *habeas corpus,* or the arrest of a citizen, except in aid of the judicial power. He certainly does not faithfully execute the laws if he takes upon himself legislative power by suspending the writ of *habeas corpus,* and the judicial power also, by arresting and imprisoning a person without due process of law. Nor can any argument be drawn from the nature of sovereignty, or the necessity of Government for self-defense in times of tumult and danger. The Government of the United States is one of delegated and limited powers. It derives its existence and authority altogether from the Constitution, and neither of its branches, executive, legislative or judicial, can exercise any of the powers of Government beyond those specified and granted. For the tenth article of the Amendments to the Constitution in express terms provides that "the powers not delegated to the United States by the Constitution, nor prohibited by it to the States, are reserved to the States respectively, or to the people."

Indeed, the security against imprisonment by executive authority, provided for in the fifth article of the Amendments to the Constitution, which I have before quoted, is nothing more than a copy of a like provision in the English Constitution, which had been firmly established before the Declaration of Independence.

Blackstone states it in the following words:

"To make imprisonment lawful, it must be either by process of law from the courts of judicature or by warrant from some legal officer having authority to commit to prison" (1 Bl. Com. 137).

The people of the United Colonies, who had themselves lived under its protection while they were British subjects, were well aware of the necessity of this safeguard for their personal liberty. And no one can believe that, in framing a government intended to guard still more efficiently the rights and liberties of the citizen against executive encroachments and oppression, they would have conferred on the President a power which the history of England had proved to be dangerous and oppressive in the hands of the Crown, and which the people of England had compelled it to surrender after a long and obstinate struggle on the part of the English Executive to usurp and retain it.

The right of the subject to the benefit of the writ of *habeas*

corpus, it must be recollected, was one of the great points in
controversy during the long struggle in England between
arbitrary government and free institutions, and must therefore have strongly attracted the attention of the statesmen
engaged in framing a new, and, as they supposed, a freer
government than the one which they had thrown off by the
Revolution. From the earliest history of the common law,
if a person were imprisoned, no matter by what authority,
he had a right to the writ of *habeas corpus* to bring his case
before the King's Bench; if no specific offense were charged
against him in the warrant of commitment, he was entitled to
be forthwith discharged; and if an offense were charged
which was bailable in its character, the Court was bound to
set him at liberty on bail. The most exciting contests
between the Crown and the people of England from the time
of *Magna Charta* were in relation to the privilege of this
writ, and they continued until the passage of the statute of
31st Charles II, commonly known as the Great *Habeas Corpus*
Act. This statute put an end to the struggle, and finally and
firmly secured the liberty of the subject against the usurpa-
tion and oppression of the executive branch of the Government. It nevertheless conferred no new right upon the subject, but only secured a right already existing. For, although
the right could not justly be denied, there was often no
effectual remedy against its violation. Until the statute of
13 William III, the judges held their offices at the pleasure
of the King, and the influence which he exercised over timid,
time-serving and partisan judges often induced them, upon
some pretext or other, to refuse to discharge the party,
although entitled by law to his discharge, or delayed their
decision from time to time, so as to prolong the imprisonment of persons who were obnoxious to the King for their

political opinions, or had incurred his resentment in any other way.

The great and inestimable value of the *habeas corpus* act of the 31st Charles II. is that it contains provisions which compel courts and judges, and all parties concerned, to perform their duties promptly in the manner specified in the statute.

A passage in Blackstone's Commentaries, showing the ancient state of the law on this subject, and the abuses which were practised through the power and influence of the Crown, and a short extract from Hallam's "Constitutional History," stating the circumstances which gave rise to the passage of this statute, explain briefly, but fully, all that is material to this subject.

Blackstone says : " To assert an absolute exemption from imprisonment in all cases is inconsistent with every idea of law and political society, and, in the end, would destroy all civil liberty by rendering its protection impossible.

" But the glory of the English law consists in clearly defining the times, the causes and the extent, when, wherefore and to what degree the imprisonment of the subject may be lawful. This it is which induces the absolute necessity of expressing upon every commitment the reason for which it is made, that the court upon a *habeas corpus* may examine into its validity, and, according to the circumstances of the case, may discharge, admit to bail, or remand the prisoner.

" And yet, early in the reign of Charles I, the Court of King's Bench, relying on some arbitrary precedents (and those, perhaps, misunderstood), determined that they would not, upon a *habeas corpus*, either bail or deliver a prisoner, though committed without any cause assigned, in case he was committed by the special command of the King, or by the Lords of the Privy Council. This drew on a Parliamentary inquiry and produced the Petition of Right—3 Charles I.—which recites this illegal judgment, and enacts that no freeman hereafter shall be so imprisoned or detained. But when, in the following year, Mr. Selden and others were committed by the Lords of the Council, in pursuance of His Majesty's special command, under a general charge of ' notable contempts, and stirring up sedition against the King and the Government,' the judges delayed for two terms (including also the long vacation) to deliver an opinion how far such a charge was bailable. And when at length they agreed that it was, they, however, annexed a condition of finding sureties for their good behavior, which still protracted their imprisonment, the Chief Justice, Sir Nicholas Hyde, at the same time declaring that ' if they were again remanded for that cause, perhaps the court would not afterwards grant a *habeas corpus*, being already made acquainted with the cause of the imprisonment.' But this was heard with indignation and astonishment by every lawyer present, according to Mr. Selden's own account of the matter, whose resentment was not cooled at the distance of four-and-twenty years " (3 Bl. Com. 133, 134).

It is worthy of remark that the offenses charged against the prisoner in this case, and relied on as a justification for his arrest and imprisonment, in their nature and character, and in the loose and vague manner in which they are stated, bear a striking resemblance to those assigned in the warrant for the arrest of Mr. Selden. And yet, even at that day, the warrant was regarded as such a flagrant violation of the rights of the subject, that the delay of the time-serving judges to set him at liberty upon the *habeas corpus* issued in his behalf excited universal indignation of the bar. The extract from Hallam's " Constitutional History " is equally impressive and equally in point :

"It is a very common mistake, and that not only among foreigners, but many from whom some knowledge of our constitutional laws might be expected, to suppose that this statute of Charles II. enlarged in a great degree our liberties, and forms a sort of epoch in their history. But though a very beneficial enactment, and eminently remedial in many cases of illegal imprisonment, it introduced no new principle, nor conferred any right upon the subject. From the earliest records of the English law, no freeman could be detained in prison, except upon a criminal charge, or conviction, or for a civil debt. In the former case it was always in his power to demand of the Court of King's Bench a writ of *habeas corpus ad subjiciendum*, directed to the person detaining him in custody, by which he was enjoined to bring up the body of the prisoner with the warrant of commitment, that the court might judge of its sufficiency, and remand the party, admit him to bail, or discharge him, according to the nature of the charge. This writ issued of right, and could not be refused by the court. It was not to bestow an immunity from arbitrary imprisonment—which is abundantly provided for in *Magna Charta* (if, indeed, it is not more ancient)—that the statute of Charles II. was enacted, but to cut off the abuses by which the Government's lust of power, and the servile subtlety of the Crown lawyers, had impaired so fundamental a privilege" (3 Hallam's " Const. Hist.," 19).

While the value set upon this writ in England has been so great that the removal of the abuses which embarrassed its employment has been looked upon as almost a new grant of liberty to the subject, it is not to be wondered at that the continuance of the writ thus made effective should have been the object of the most jealous care. Accordingly, no power in England short of that of Parliament can suspend or authorize the suspension of the writ of *habeas corpus.* I quote again from Blackstone (1 Bl. Com. 136): "But the happiness of our Constitution is that it is not left to the executive power to determine when the danger of the State is so great as to render this measure expedient. It is the Parliament only, or legislative power, that, whenever it sees proper, can authorize the Crown, by suspending the *habeas corpus* for a short and limited time, to imprison suspected persons without giving any reason for so doing." If the President of the United States may suspend the writ, then the Constitution of the United States has conferred upon him more regal and absolute power over the liberty of the citizen than the people of England have thought it safe to entrust to the Crown—a power which the Queen of England cannot exercise at this day, and which could not have been lawfully exercised by the sovereign even in the reign of Charles I.

But I am not left to form my judgment upon this great question from analogies between the English Government and our own, or the commentaries of English jurists, or the decisions of English courts, although upon this subject they are entitled to the highest respect, and are justly regarded and received as authoritative by our courts of justice. To guide me to a right conclusion, I have the Commentaries on the Constitution of the United States of the late Mr. Justice Story, not only one of the most eminent jurists of the age, but for a long time one of the brightest ornaments of the Supreme Court of the United States, and also the clear and authoritative decision of that court itself, given more than half a century since, and conclusively establishing the principles I have above stated.

Mr. Justice Story, speaking in his Commentaries of the *habeas corpus* clause in the Constitution, says : " It is obvious that cases of a peculiar emergency may arise which may justify, nay, even require, the temporary suspension of any right to the writ. But as it has frequently happened in foreign countries, and even in England, that the writ has, upon various pretexts and occasions, been suspended, whereby persons apprehended upon suspicion have suffered a long imprisonment, sometimes from design, and sometimes because they were forgotten, the right to suspend it is expressly confined to cases of rebellion or invasion, where the public safety may require it. A very just and wholesome restraint, which cuts down at a blow a fruitful means of oppression, capable of being abused in bad times to the worst of purposes. Hitherto no suspension of the writ has ever been authorized by Congress since the establishment of the Constitution. It would seem, as the power is given to Congress to suspend the writ of *habeas corpus* in cases of rebellion or invasion, that the right to judge whether the exigency had arisen must exclusively belong to that body " (3 Story's Com. on the Constitution, Section 1836).

And Chief Justice Marshall, in delivering the opinion of the Supreme Court in the case of *ex parte* Bollman and Swartwout, uses this decisive language in 4 Cranch 95 : " It may be worthy of remark that this Act (speaking of the one under which I am proceeding) was passed by the first Congress of the United States, sitting under a Constitution which had declared 'that the privilege of the writ of *habeas corpus* should not be suspended unless when, in cases of rebellion or invasion, the public safety might require it.' Acting under the immediate influence of this injunction, they must have felt with peculiar force the obligation of providing

efficient means by which this great constitutional privilege
should receive life and activity ; for if the means be not in
existence, the privilege itself would be lost, although no law
for its suspension should be enacted. Under the impression
of this obligation, they give to all the courts the power of
awarding writs of *habeas corpus."*

And again, on page 101 : " If at any time the public safety
should require the suspension of the powers vested by this
Act in the courts of the United States, it is for the Legislature to say so. That question depends on political considerations, on which the Legislature is to decide. Until
the legislative will be expressed, this court can only see its
duty, and must obey the laws."

I can add nothing to these clear and emphatic words of
my great predecessor. But the documents before me show
that the military authority in this case has gone far beyond
the mere suspension of the privilege of the writ of *habeas
corpus.* It has, by force of arms, thrust aside the judicial
authorities and officers to whom the Constitution has confided the power and duty of interpreting and administering
the laws, and substituted a military government in its place,
to be administered and executed by military officers. For,
at the time these proceedings were had against John Merryman, the district judge of Maryland, the commissioner appointed under the Act of Congress, the district attorney and
the marshal, all resided in the city of Baltimore, a few miles
only from the home of the prisoner. Up to that time there
had never been the slightest resistance or obstruction to the
process of any court or judicial officer of the United States
in Maryland, except by the military authority. And if a
military officer, or any other person, had reason to believe
that the prisoner had committed any offense against the laws

of the United States, it was his duty to give information of the fact, and the evidence to support it, to the district attorney; it would then have become the duty of that officer to bring the matter before the district judge or commissioner, and if there was sufficient legal evidence to justify his arrest, the judge or commissioner would have issued his warrant to the marshal to arrest him, and upon the hearing of the case would have held him to bail, or committed him for trial, according to the character of the offense as it appeared in the testimony, or would have discharged him immediately, if there was not sufficient evidence to support the accusation. There was no danger of any obstruction or resistance to the action of the civil authorities, and therefore no reason whatever for the interposition of the military. Yet, under these circumstances, a military officer stationed in Pennsylvania, without giving any information to the district attorney, and without any application to the judicial authorities, assumes to himself the judicial power in the District of Maryland; undertakes to decide what constitutes the crime of treason or rebellion; what evidence (if, indeed, he required any) is sufficient to support the accusation and justify the commitment; and commits the party without a hearing, even before himself, to close custody in a strongly garrisoned fort, to be there held, it would seem, during the pleasure of those who committed him.

The Constitution provides, as I have before said, that "no person shall be deprived of life, liberty or property without due process of law." It declares that "the right of the people to be secure in their persons, houses, papers and effects against unreasonable searches and seizures shall not be violated, and no warrant shall issue, but upon probable cause, supported by oath or affirmation, and particularly describing the place to be searched, and the persons or things to be seized." It provides that the party accused shall be entitled to a speedy trial in a court of justice.

These great and fundamental laws, which Congress itself could not suspend, have been disregarded and suspended, like the writ of *habeas corpus,* by a military order, supported by force of arms. Such is the case now before me, and I can only say that if the authority which the Constitution has confided to the judiciary department and judicial officers may thus upon any pretext or under any circumstances be usurped by the military power at its discretion, the people of the United States are no longer living under a government of laws, but every citizen holds life, liberty and property at the will and pleasure of the army officer in whose military district he may happen to be found.

In such a case my duty was too plain to be mistaken. I have exercised all the power which the Constitution and laws confer upon me, but that power has been resisted by a force too strong for me to overcome. It is possible that the officer who has incurred this grave responsibility may have misunderstood his instructions and exceeded the authority intended to be given him. I shall therefore order all the proceedings in this case, with my opinion, to be filed and recorded in the Circuit Court of the United States for the District of Maryland, and direct the clerk to transmit a copy, under seal, to the President of the United States. It will then remain for that high officer, in fulfilment of his constitutional obligation, to "take care that the laws be faithfully executed," to determine what measures he will take to cause the civil process of the United States to be respected and enforced.

R. B. TANEY,
Chief Justice of the Supreme Court
of the United States.

APPENDIX IV.

On the 12th of July, 1861, I sent a message to the First and Second Branches of the City Council referring to the events of the 19th of April and those which followed. The first paragraph and the concluding paragraphs of this document are here inserted:

" THE MAYOR'S MESSAGE.

" To the Honorable the Members of the
FIRST AND SECOND BRANCHES OF THE CITY COUNCIL.

"*Gentlemen:*—A great object of the reform movement was to separate municipal affairs entirely from national politics, and in accordance with this principle I have heretofore, in all my communications to the city council, carefully refrained from any allusion to national affairs. I shall not now depart from this rule further than is rendered absolutely necessary by the unprecedented condition of things at present existing in this city. . . . .

" After the board of police had been superseded, and its members arrested by the order of General Banks, I proposed, in order to relieve the serious complication which had arisen, to proceed, as the only member left free to act, to exercise the power of the board as far as an individual member could do so. Marshal Kane, while he objected to the propriety of this course, was prepared to place his resignation in my hands whenever I should request it, and the majority of the board interposed no objection to my pursuing such course as I might deem it right and proper to adopt in view of the existing circumstances, and upon my own responsibility, until the board should be enabled to resume the exercise of its functions.

"If this arrangement could have been effected, it would have continued in the exercise of their duties the police force which is lawfully enrolled, and which has won the confidence and applause of all good citizens by its fidelity and impartiality at all times and under all circumstances. But the arrangement was not satisfactory to the Federal authorities.

"As the men of the police force, through no fault of theirs, are now prevented from discharging their duty, their pay constitutes a legal claim on the city from which, in my opinion, it cannot be relieved.

"The force which has been enrolled is in direct violation of the law of the State, and no money can be appropriated by the city for its support without incurring the heavy penalties provided by the Act of Assembly.

"Officers in the Fire Alarm and Police Telegraph Department who are appointed by the mayor and city council, and not by the board of police, have been discharged and others have been substituted in their place.

"I mention these facts with profound sorrow, and with no purpose whatever of increasing the difficulties unfortunately existing in this city, but because it is your right to be acquainted with the true condition of affairs, and because I cannot help entertaining the hope that redress will yet be afforded by the authorities of the United States upon a proper representation made by you. I am entirely satisfied that the suspicion entertained of any meditated hostility on the part of the city authorities against the General Government is wholly unfounded, and with the best means of knowledge express the confident belief and conviction that there is no organization of any kind among the people for such a purpose. I have no doubt that the officers of the United States have acted on information which they deemed reliable, obtained from our own citizens, some of whom may be deluded by their fears, while others are actuated by baser motives; but suspicions thus derived can, in my judgment, form no sufficient justification for what I deem to be grave and alarming violations of the rights of individual citizens of the city of Baltimore and of the State of Maryland.

"Very respectfully,

"Geo. Wm. Brown, *Mayor.*"

APPENDIX V.

As a part of the history of the times, it may not be inappropriate to reproduce an account, taken from the Baltimore *American* of December 5, 1860, of the reception of the Putnam Phalanx of Hartford, Connecticut, in the city of Baltimore. At this time it still seemed to most men of moderate views that the impending troubles might be averted through concessions and compromise. In the tone of the two speeches, both of which were, of course, meant to be friendly and conciliatory, there is a difference to be noted which was, I think, characteristic of the attitude of the two sections; in the one speech some prominence is given to the Constitution and constitutional rights; in the other, loyalty to the Union is the theme enforced:

"The Putnam Phalanx of Hartford, Connecticut, under the command of Major Horace Goodwin, yesterday afternoon reached here, at four o'clock, by the Philadelphia train, *en route* for a visit to the tomb of Washington. A detachment of the Eagle Artillery gave them a national salute.

"The Battalion Baltimore City Guards, consisting of four companies, under the command of Major Joseph P. Warner, were drawn up on Broadway, and after passing in salute, the column moved by way of Broadway and Baltimore and Calvert streets to the old Universalist church-building.

"As soon as the military entered the edifice and were seated, the galleries were thrown open to the public, and in a few minutes they were crowded to overflowing.

"Captain Parks introduced Major Goodwin to Mayor Brown, who was in turn introduced to the commissioned officers of the Phalanx. Major Goodwin then turned to his command and said: 'Gentlemen of the Phalanx, I have the honor of introducing you to the Mayor of the city of Baltimore.' Mayor Brown arose, and after bowing to the Battalion, addressed them as follows:

"MAYOR BROWN'S SPEECH.

"'*Mr. Commander and Gentlemen:*—In the name and on behalf of the people of Baltimore, I extend to the Putnam Phalanx a sincere and hearty welcome to the hospitalities of our city. The citizens of Baltimore are always glad to receive visits from the citizen-soldiers of sister States, because they come as friends, and more than friends—as the defenders of a common country.

"'These sister States, as we love to call them, live somewhat far apart, and gradually become more and more separated by distance, just as sisters will be as the children marry and one by one leave the parent homestead.

"'But, gentlemen, far or near, on the Connecticut or Potomac, on the Gulf of Mexico or the great lakes, on the Atlantic or Pacific, they are sisters still, united by blood and affection, and the holy tie should never be severed. (Applause.)

"'Let me carry the figure a step further, and add what I know will meet with a response from the Putnam Phalanx, with whose history and high character I am somewhat acquainted—that a sisterhood of States, like separate families of sisters living in the same neighborhood, can never dwell together in peace unless each is permitted to manage her own domestic affairs in her own way (applause); not only without active interference from the rest, but even without much fault-finding or advice, however well intended it may be.

"'Maryland has sometimes been called the Heart State, because she lies very close to the great heart of the Union; and she might also be called the Heart State because her heart beats with true and warm love for the Union. (Loud applause.) Nor, as I trust, does Connecticut fall short of her in this respect. And when the questions now before the country come to be fairly understood, and the people look into them with their own eyes, and take matters into their own hands, I believe that we shall see a sight of which politicians, North and South, little dream. (Applause.) We shall see whether there is a love for the Union or not.

"'But there are great national questions agitating the land which must now be finally settled. One is, Will the States of the North keep on their statute-books laws which violate a right of the States of the South, guaranteed to them by the Constitution of the United States? No individuals, no families, no States, can live in peace together when any right of a part is persistently and deliberately violated by the rest. Another question is, What shall be done with the national territory? Shall it belong exclusively to the North or the South, or shall it be shared by both, as it was gained by the blood and treasure of both? Are there not wisdom and patriotism enough in the land to settle these questions?

"'Gentlemen, your presence here to-day proves that you are animated by a higher and larger sentiment than that of State pride—the sentiment of American nationality. The most sacred spot in America is the tomb of Washington, and to that shrine you are about to make a pilgrimage. You come from a State celebrated above all others for the most extensive diffusion of the great blessing of education; which has a colonial and Revolutionary history abounding in honorable memorials; which has heretofore done her full share in founding the institutions of this country—the land of Washington—and which can now do as much as any other in preserving that land one and undivided, as it was left by the Father of his Country. I will not permit myself to doubt that your State and our State, that Connecticut and Maryland, will both be on the same side, as they have often been in times past, and that they will both respect and obey and uphold the sacred Constitution of the country.' (Shouts of applause.)

" As soon as the Mayor concluded, Major Goodwin arose; but it was some time before he could be heard, such was the tremendous applause with which he was greeted. The Major is nearly ninety years of age, and is one of the most venerable-looking men in the country. Dressed in the old Revolutionary uniform, a *fac-simile* of that worn by General Putnam, and with his locks silvered with age, we may say that his appearance electrified the multitude, and shout after shout shook the very building. Major Goodwin expressed himself as follows :

" ' Mr. Mayor and gentlemen of the Baltimore City Guards, permit me to introduce to you our Judge Advocate, Captain Stuart.'

" Captain Stuart arose and spoke as follows :

" SPEECH OF CAPTAIN STUART.

" ' Your Honor, Mayor Brown: For your kind words of welcome, and for your patriotic sentiments in favor of the Union, the Putnam Phalanx returns you its most cordial thanks. I can assure you, sir, that when you spoke in such eloquent terms of the value and importance of a united country, you but echoed the sentiments of the whole of our

organization ; and let me say, it is with great pleasure, upon
a journey, as we are, to the tomb of the illustrious Washington, that we pause for a while within a city so famed for
its intelligence, its industry, its general opulence and its
courtesy, as is this your own beautiful Baltimore.

" ' We opine, nay, we know from what you have yourself,
in such fitting terms, just expressed, that you heartily appreciate the purpose which lies at the foundation of our organization, that purpose being the lofty one of commemorating,
by our military attire and discipline, the imposing foundation-
period of the American Republic, of attracting our own
patriotic feeling, and that of all who may honor us with their
observation, to the exalted virtues of those heroic men who
laid the foundations of our present national prosperity and
glory—men of whom your city and State furnished, as it
pleasantly happens, a large and most honorable share.

" ' We come, sir, from that portion of the United States in
which the momentous struggle for American freedom took its
rise, and where the blood of its earliest martyrs was shed ;
from the region where odious writs of assistance, infamous
Courts of Admiralty, intolerable taxation, immolated charters
of government and prohibited commerce were once fast
paving the way for the slavery of our institutions ; from the
region of a happy and God-fearing people—from the region,
sir, of Lexington and Concord and Bunker Hill and Croton
Heights, of ravaged New London and fired Fairfield and
Norwalk and devastated Danbury and sacked New Haven.
And we come, Mr. Mayor, to a city and State, we are
proudly aware, which to all these trials and perils of assaulted New England, and to the trials and perils of our
whole common country, during "the times that tried men's
souls," gave ever the meed of its heartfelt sympathy, and the

unstinted tribute of its patriotic blood and treasure ; which, with a full and clear comprehension of all the great prin- ciples of American freedom, and a devotion to those principles that was ever ardent and exalted, signalized themselves by their wisdom in council and their prowess on the field.

" ' When the devoted metropolis of New England began to feel the awful scourge of the Writ Bill, Maryland it was that then contributed most liberal supplies for its suffering people, and with these supplies those cheering, ever-to-be-remembered, talismanic words : " The Supreme Director of all events will terminate this severe trial of your patriotism in the happy confirmation of American freedom."

" ' When this same metropolis soon after became the seat of war, Maryland it was that at once sent to the camp around Boston her own companies of " dauntless riflemen," under her brave Michael Cresap and the gallant Price, to mingle in the defense of New England firesides and New England homes. She saw and felt, and bravely uttered at the time, the fact that in the then existing state of public affairs there was no alternative left for her, or for the country at large, but " base submission or manly resistance "; and, Mr. Mayor, at the memorable battle of Long Island she made this manly resist- ance, for there she poured out the life-blood of no less than two hundred and fifty-nine of her gallant sons, who fought in her own Smallwood's immortal regiment; and elsewhere, from the St. Lawrence to the banks of the Savannah, through Pennsylvania, Virginia and both the Carolinas—devoted the best blood within her borders, and the flower of her soldiery, to the battlefields of the Union.

" ' Sir, we of this Phalanx recall these and other Revolu- tionary memories belonging to your city and State with pride and satisfaction. They unite Connecticut and Maryland in strong and pleasant bonds. And we are highly gratified to be here in the midst of them, and to receive at your hands so grateful a welcome as that which you have extended.

"'Be assured, Mr. Mayor, that in the sentiments of devotion to our common country which you so eloquently express, this Phalanx sympathizes heart and soul. You may plant the flag of the Union anywhere and we shall warm to it. And now, renewedly thanking you for the present manifestation of courtesy, we shall leave to enjoy the hospitality which awaits us in pleasant quarters at our hotel.'

"Captain Stuart was frequently interrupted by applause."

APPENDIX VI.

On the 19th of April, 1880, a portion of the members of the Sixth Massachusetts Regiment again visited Baltimore, and an account of its reception, taken from the Baltimore *Sun* and the Baltimore *American,* seems to be a fitting close to this paper :

"Thirty-nine members of the Association of Survivors of the Sixth Massachusetts Union Regiment came to Baltimore yesterday afternoon, to celebrate the nineteenth anniversary of their march through Baltimore, April 19, 1861, which gave rise to the riot of that day. The visitors were met, on landing from the cars at President-street Depot, by Wilson, Dushane and Harry Howard Posts, Grand Army of the Republic, in full uniform, with band and drum corps. The line was up Broadway to Baltimore street, to Barnum's Hotel. A file of policemen, with Marshals Gray and Frey, kept the street open for the parade. The streets were crowded with people. The Massachusetts men wore citizen's dress and badges."

Wilson Post No. 1, of the Grand Army of the Republic, received the visitors in their hall, Rialto Building, at two o'clock. Commander Dukehart, of Wilson Post, welcomed the guests in a brief speech, and then introduced Comrade Crowley, of the old Sixth, who said :

"'Nineteen years ago I was but a boy. A few days before the 19th of April, the militia of Middlesex County were summoned for the defense of the National Capital. We left workshops, desk and family, to come to the defense of the capital. We thought we were coming to a picnic ; that the

people of South Carolina were a little off their balance, and
would be all right on sober second thought. A few miles
out from Baltimore the Quartermaster gave us each ten
rounds of ammunition. We had been singing songs. The
Colonel told us he expected trouble in Baltimore, and impressed on each man not to fire until he was compelled to.
The singing ceased, and we then thought we had serious
business before us, and that others besides South Carolina
had lost their balance. When we reached the Baltimore
Depot some of the cars had gone ahead, and four companies—
young men—were in the cars unconscious of what was going
on outside. We thought the people of Baltimore and Maryland were of the same Government, and if not they ought to
be. (Cheers and applause.) That they had the same
interest in the Government, the best ever devised; that
Maryland at least was loyal. A man knocked on the car-
door and told us they were tearing up the track. Our
Captain said, " Men, file out!" The order was given and we
marched out. The Captain said, " March as close as you possibly can. Fire on no man unless compelled." We marched
through railroad iron, bricks and other missiles. We proved
ourselves brave soldiers—proved that we could wait, at least,
for the word of command. We were pelted in Baltimore
nineteen years ago. We lost some of our comrades, and
others were disabled for life. But we went to Washington.
We don't claim to be the saviors of the capital; we take no
great credit for what we did; but we did the best we could,
and the result is shown. The success of our march through
Baltimore to-day is as indelibly fixed and will ever be as
fresh as that of nineteen years ago, and our reception will
remain in our hearts and minds as long as life lasts. My
father had six sons, and five were at the front at the same

time. I had learned to think that if Maryland, South Carolina or Virginia was to declare independence the Government
would be broken up, and that we would have no country, no
home, no flag. We were not fighting for Massachusetts, for
Maryland or for Virginia, but for our country—the United
States (cheers and applause)—remembering the declaration of
the great statesman, "Liberty and Union, now and forever,
one and inseparable." This country went through four years
of carnage and blood. Few families, North or South, but
have mourning at their firesides; but it was not in vain, for
it has established the fact that we are one people, and are an
all-powerful people. (Prolonged cheers.) Our reception
to-day has convinced us that the war has ended, and that
there are Union men in Maryland as in Massachusetts;
that we are brothers, and will be so to the end of time;
that this is one great country; and that the people are
marching on in amity and power, second to none on the face
of the globe.' (Cheers.)

"In the evening there was a banquet at the Eutaw House,
and Judge Geo. William Brown, who was Mayor of Baltimore in 1861, presided. Nearly two hundred persons were
at table. After the dinner was over, Judge Brown said:

"'This is the 19th of April, a day memorable in the annals
of this city, and in the annals of the country. It is filled in
my mind with the most painful recollections of my life, and
I doubt not that many who are here present share with me
those feelings. I shall make but brief allusions to the
events of that day. The city authorities of Baltimore of
that time have mostly passed away, and I believe I am the
only one here present to-night. In justice to the living and
the dead I have to say that the authorities of Baltimore
faithfully endeavored to do their duty. It is not necessary for me, perhaps, to say so in this presence. (Applause.)

It was not their fault that the Massachusetts Sixth Regiment met a bloody reception in the streets of Baltimore. The visit of that regiment on both occasions has a great and important significance. What did it mean in 1861? It meant civil war; that the irrepressible conflict which Mr. Seward predicted had broken out at last, and that, as Mr. Lincoln said, a house divided against itself cannot stand. A great question then presented itself to the country. When war virtually began in Baltimore, by bloodshed on both sides, it meant that the question must be settled by force whether or not the house should stand. It took four years of war, waged with indomitable perseverance, to decide it, because the combatants on both sides were sustained by deep and honest convictions. It is not surprising, looking back coolly and calmly on the feelings of that day, that they found vent as they did. I am not here to excuse or to apologize, but to acknowledge facts. That was the significance of the first visit of the Massachusetts Sixth Regiment, in response to the call of the President of the United States. After the war there was peace. But enforced peace is not sufficient in a family of States any more than in a household. There must be among brothers respect, confidence, mutual help and forbearance, and, above everything, justice and right. After nineteen years the visit of survivors of the Sixth Massachusetts is, I hope, significant of more than peace. It is, I hope, significant of the fact that there is a true bond of union between the North and the South (applause), and that we are a family of States, all equal, all friends; and if it be, there is no one in the country who can more fervently thank God than myself that the old house still stands.' (Applause.)

"Judge Brown offered as a toast: 'The Sixth Regiment of Massachusetts: Baltimore extends to her fraternal greeting.'"

INDEX.

A

Acton, regiment mustered in, 42.

Allen, E. J., dispatches addressed to, 131.

American, The, on the Baltimore riot of 1861, 65; account of the Putnam Phalanx in Baltimore, 160 –167 ; on the reception of the Sixth Massachusetts Regiment in Baltimore, 167–170.

Andrew, Gov. J. A., correspondence with Mayor Brown, 54, 55.

Arkansas, secession of, 33.

B

Baltimore, unjust prejudice against, 13, 19 ; supposed conspiracy in, 14, 15, 120 ; slaveholders in, 30 ; Sixth Massachusetts Regiment in, 42–53, 167–170 ; excitement on 20th April, 60, 61, 64 ; defense of, 63 ; apprehension of bloodshed in, 75 ; armed neutrality, 77 ; Gen. Butler's entrance into, 84 ; Gen. Dix's headquarters in, 100, 101 ; Mayor's message to City Council, 157–159 ; reception of Putnam Phalanx in, 160–166.

Banks, Gen. N. P., in command, 97 ; arrests police commissioners of Baltimore, 98, 99 ; Secretary Cameron's letter to, 102 ; General McClellan's letter to, 102.

Bartol, Judge, imprisonment of, 94.

Belger, Major, comes to Baltimore, 73.

Bell, Presidential vote for, 25.

Black, Judge, on martial law, 93.

Blackstone on the right of imprisonment, 147, 149.

Bond's, Judge, errand to Lincoln, 57, 61.

Boston, slave-traffic in, 20 ; regiment mustered in, 42.

Brand, Rev. William F., efforts for emancipation, 113.

Breckinridge, Presidential vote for, 25.

Brown, Geo. Wm., meets the Massachusetts Sixth in Baltimore, 48, 49 ; Captain Dike on, 54 ; correspondence with Gov. Andrew, 54, 55 ; speech to the excited public, 56 ; writes to President Lincoln about passage of troops through Baltimore, 57, 61, 62 ; interview with President Lincoln, 71–75 ; General Butler's letter to, 83, 84 ; petitions Congress to restore peace to city, 99 ; arrest of, 102, 103, 108 ; correspondence with General Dix, 104–108 ; parole offered to, 110, 111 ; anti-slavery principles of, 113 ; opposed to secession, 115 ; on the tendencies of the age, 117, 118 ; message to City Council, 157–159 ; speech to the Putnam Phalanx, 160–163 ; speech to the survivors of the Sixth Massachusetts Regiment, 169, 170.